SOME DAY I'M GOING TO FLY

Hilary McDowell is a dramatist, journalist, performance
poet, counsellor, and psychologist. At present director of
the Multi-Media Workshop in Belfast, she is a Deaconess
of the Presbyterian Church in Ireland, exercising a
ministry of outreach and reconciliation with all the
denominations through drama, art, and music. Severely
disabled from birth, Hilary represents Northern Ireland on
the European Community Commission for Arts and
Disability.

D0543400

SOME
DAY
I'M
GOING
TO
FLY

Hilary McDowell

TRi△NGLE

First published 1995
Triangle
SPCK
Holy Trinity Church
Marylebone Road
London NW1 4DU

British Library Cataloguing-in-Publication Data
A catalogue record for this book is available from the British Library.
ISBN 0-281-04801-0

Typeset by Rowland Phototypesetting Ltd,
Bury St Edmunds, Suffolk
Printed and bound in Great Britain by
BPC Paperbacks Ltd
Member of The British Printing Company Ltd

To my mother, and in memory of my father

Contents

Poems

Foreword

The first important thing you notice about Hilary McDowell is that she is disabled. The second important thing you notice is that she is not. I have always laughed at some of the more extreme examples of Politically Correct language, but perhaps there is something to be said for describing someone like Hilary as 'Differently Abled'. If ever spirit and personality transfigured a human being, they do in the case of this lively Belfast lady.

My wife Bridget and I first met Hilary at the Carberry Towers Christian Arts Festival near Edinburgh, an annual event for families that we have always greatly enjoyed. When a tiny Irish person took centre stage one evening we were a little worried. With people who perform their own poetry there is always a ghastly possibility that we, the audience, will have to perform with more vigour, conviction and concentration than the poet. When you add a high degree of physical disability to the situation, members of the audience almost tie themselves in knots as they attempt to convey warm, deeply sincere appreciation. Yes, all right, it's pathetic and it shouldn't be like that, but that's what happens. It didn't happen on this occasion. Hilary was superb. She charmed me. She made me cry. She made me laugh. She made me decide to major on prose.

Later, during the same week, Hilary and I appeared together as David and Goliath at one of the morning worship sessions. The little sketch that we did was devised and forced into life by Hilary, and was a tremendous success with our mixed-age audience. I played a cultured, over-emotional Goliath, while Hilary was a very endearing David in a helmet that was much too big for him (her), who ended up being carried away in the arms of the reformed giant. It was an inspired piece of theatre, and she inspired it.

Since that occasion we have met Hilary a couple of times in her home city of Belfast, and she has stayed with us in our house near the South Downs in Sussex. These more leisurely encounters have given us the chance to hear about her faith, which is Jesus-centred and uncompromising, and her life story, which is an extraordinary combination of great blessing and continual suffering. I think Hilary likes to think of herself as a simple soul with a simple outlook, but I don't think she is that at all. She is a very complex personality who has overcome numberless hurdles, and, in the process, developed a strength of will and purpose that God is using increasingly to convey not just his warmth and compassion, but also the granular nature of his dealings with men and women. Her writing and her performances touch people on a very deep level.

I am so glad that you are about to meet her through this book.

ADRIAN PLASS

Preface

Autobiographies, as a rule, start at the beginning, move to the middle, and more or less finish at the end – or as near to an end as the author can achieve without actually dying.

This is not an autobiography; it is an album of 'flashbulb memory', vivid-freeze photos in the mind which stamp themselves for ever on the palmprint of the soul; events that have given birth to a poem. I believe it is at the level of poetry that we see most clearly into an author's heart, so I thank you for allowing me to share mine with you. Each person bears a heartbeat whose pattern has been influenced by numerous circumstances. As a committed Christian and qualified Deaconess, it is a great privilege to be able to share the gospel of Christ throughout Ireland, both north and south. Working alongside every denomination in the striving for peace in our land, I exercise a lay ministry of the Protestant tradition within the mainstream Presbyterian denomination in the Province.

My vocation as Director of the Multi-Media Workshop takes me all over Ireland, and also involves much travel throughout Europe and beyond. It is great to travel, but it is wonderful to come home to Belfast, where I live with my mother who has been a widow since 1978. This is my immediate family, but the family circle extends much further. By driving only 12 miles to the seaside town of Bangor, I can visit my sister Dorothy, her husband John, and their teenage children, Alan and Julie. Auntie Ellie, my mother's sister, lives only 1 mile away from our home in Belfast. Of the five remaining aunts on my father's side (sadly, one died last year), three live to the north side of Belfast, and two emigrated to

Australia many years ago. I dare not attempt to name the many cousins I have been privileged to inherit, several of whom I see often and are cherished friends.

Numbering outwards from these folk would be impossible. My mind boggles when I realise how many people God has brought within my work's sphere of reference. In one decade alone during the 1980s, over eleven thousand people have participated in the training and scope of the Multi-Media Workshop, availing themselves of the teaching, preaching, dramatising, art, music, and counselling facilities provided full time by myself, and the voluntary spare-time teams who have trained with us, and with whom I now have the pleasure of working.

Considering that the parameters of my 'family' are limitless, reference to many people has to be omitted. The events recorded here are not necessarily the most important ones, nor the least. They are, however, pictures that will not go away.

If you are reading this and we know each other, either much or little, please do not be offended if you are not mentioned. You might not be included here because the flashbulb wasn't working that day, or, on the other hand, because the photo it took is one that I am still developing, close to my heart.

If we have not met and you are visiting my memories for the first time in this book, I hope some of these mind photos will help you to sort out your own album – not in the darkroom, but in God's light.

Acknowledgements

Biblical quotations are taken from the following versions: Authorized Version (King James Version) (the text of the Authorized Version of the Bible is the property of the Crown in perpetuity, reproduced by permission of the Crown's Patentee, Cambridge University Press) and the Revised Standard Version of the Bible © 1946, 1952, 1971 by the Division of Christian Education of the National Council of the Churches of Christ in the USA. Used by permission.

My thanks to Bridget and Adrian Plass, and Michele Guinness, for their encouragement towards the writing of this book.

FLIGHT PATH

Some folk live their lives
Gaze welded to the pavement.
Me, I stumble on
Eye level to the distant horizon,
Someday, I'm going to fly!

1 ARRIVING

Designer babies would not have welcomed me into their club. Born at a very early age, I don't remember much about the event. Perhaps that is just as well, considering that I entered the world with a body folded in two. Toes doubled up to nose, and these two sections as difficult to prise apart as a pair of rusty scissors. Feet curled in a little ball, toes tucked underneath and stuck to the heels, unable to straighten. Jaw broken and mangled by a forceps birth. Lower limbs dislocated beyond locomotion possibilities, and a general assortment of internal organs dysfunctioning. They say all babies are beautiful – with facial deformity, muscle paralyses, hearing loss, and sight abnormality, I must have looked a 'pretty' pink parcel of parody.

But I'd arrived! Dangerously premature and boasting seven handicaps, I was laid into my mother's arms. I'm sure the first sound that I heard was sobbing: my cries for breath, hers for God. It was a good start, and one that would prepare me well for the uphill struggle of life, and the incredible view from the top of the climb.

Not surprisingly, my mother asked the doctors, 'What'll I do?' They told her only one thing: 'Take her home.' There was no other answer they could give. The prognosis was that I would not walk, and might not speak. 'Love her,' they said, 'you won't have her for very long.' In those first early weeks and months of life, only my parents could testify to the trauma and the pain. Three weeks was the doctors' original attempt at predicting my life expectancy. Fortunately, for me, they were wrong.

The normal sleepless nights that new parents experience

were, in this case, greatly compounded. Food could only be taken a few sips at a sitting, and I had to be fed every hour. How do you feed a child whose mouth only opens a hair's breadth? Who cannot swallow properly or digest food? The normal feeding implements were useless. No amount of searching could find a bottle teat that would fit the tiny aperture. In desperation, my mother bought a new fountain pen and sterilised the ink dropper. I think that before she was finished, she also had to use it at the other end of me to ease the pain.

'What happens,' Mum asked the doctors, 'if I oversleep and miss giving her a feed?' 'She won't be here in the morning,' was the stark reply. Between them, Mum and Dad kept the rota flawless, and the baby thrived to become a toddler with an incredible pair of lungs and an unprecedented talent for voice projection, but no toddling.

I do not remember when I first discovered a mirror; but as an adult, whenever I have a 'Monday-morning blues' experience in front of my reflection, I read again the poem I wrote on the back of my mirror at home:

MIRROR-IMAGE

Any complaints about this particular model
Should be referred directly to the maker.

Our mirror-image is the image of God seeded within our souls, regardless of the shape of the flesh-tent that clothes us. As he told Jeremiah: 'Before I formed you in the womb I knew you, and before you were born I consecrated you' (Jeremiah 1.5).

Touched in the womb – and God does not make mistakes. Whatever aspect of a fallen earth contributed to the accident of nature which produced seven handicaps for my life-challenge, I know that God's creative touch in the womb turned darkness to light, negative to positive, despair to challenge. I have learnt from hard experience that it is not what happens to us that makes or breaks us, but what we do with it.

Given back to God, any negatives can be transformed into the positive which he had originally intended for the person concerned. In my experience, he fulfils his potential for our lives, not necessarily by removing the difficulties, but by climbing inside them with us and transforming the situation from within.

FAITH IS CLIMBING WITH CUT KNEES

Born to the planet in the belly of hopelessness—
Nothing extinguishes light,
Children of darkness surrender to meaninglessness—
Watch me birthed hard for the fight,
Let those with soft shoes feel black satin on tarmac,
Denied the joy of the climb,
But teeth-clenched and bleeding to rock-strewn summits,
I'll prove God's strength till I die.

2 'WOULDN'T THE WHEELS GET STUCK IN THE UNDERGROWTH?'

We prayed for eight years. I knew I would walk one day; the only unknown was the date. God's presence had always been a constant reality; he was as real to me as the parents who loved him and myself with consistent fervour. No undue pressure was put on me to walk. What I experienced was constant love and attention, and endless effort by both parents to keep me active and stimulated.

Mum would faithfully invent new exercises for my legs, and turn the tedious repetition into games to keep me interested. Laughter accompanied each leg lifting and dropping session as hour after hour, day after day, she made funny faces and tickled and cajoled as each lifeless foot was raised in her hands and dropped again on to the soft cushion. Then there was the 'crawling' game. Tied on to Mum's back with a cushion and a strap, I would ride around the dining-room as Mum crawled on all fours across the floor, pushing a ball in front with her head, encouraging, 'Get the ball, Hilary'. I was well past the normal toddling age, and too heavy for her back before this game stopped.

Dad's 'wrestling' sessions were great fun too. The exercise built up strong arm muscles, and taught me that a passive view of the world was not on the agenda for any McDowell worth her salt.

I went everywhere, for the maxim in our family was, 'If Hilary can't go with us, we won't go.' In those days, when children were expected to be seen and not heard (and, in most cases, a disabled child was expected to stay by the fireside and knit), I was taken into every social situation possible.

At the age of five, I was one of the first multiply-disabled children in Northern Ireland to be admitted to a 'normal' primary school, thanks to the vision of Mr Hunniford, Principal of Springfield Road Primary school in Belfast, and the teachers there. Carried by Mum up and down the two long flights of stone steps each day and eased in and out of my wooden desk-seat, I wondered when God would put me on my feet. I knew he would – I just didn't know when. Meantime, once a week, Daddy carried me to the vestry of our church, Woodvale Presbyterian, where the minister, Reverend R. G. Craig, and the elders prayed for my healing.

It was Mr Craig who baptised me. He tells me that two babies were baptised that day: myself, and a strong, able-bodied boy. Sadly, the little boy died a short time later.

Some time before my eighth birthday, I realised that the personal relationship I had with Jesus from birth would have to be made 'official'. I knew it was time to commit my life to him in a conscious way, no longer taking him for granted. One evening in my bedroom, I made the decision to accept him as Lord and Saviour. Until then, Jesus had been a friend; but now I surrendered my life, and he became, also, a loving Master.

At first, I wondered if I ought to be kneeling as I prayed for forgiveness for my sins, but as I considered the impossibility of making unformed knee joints bend, I felt God's warmth enclose me like a huge blanket and I began to laugh and laugh. It was as though he was laughing too, and sharing the private joke with me. I knew that 'all things are possible with God', and suddenly realised that if kneeling was necessary, he would see to it. Since he had not, I reckoned it must not be quite as essential as I had imagined.

Instead, I stretched out of bed, opened the bedside cabinet and took a piece of paper on which to draw up my own personal commitment pledge. I constructed the wording myself, and included an illustration: the cross sketched in childish 3D stretched the length of the page. Confession was there, my repentance in full. (Especially for all the hair-pulling episodes with my older sister, Dorothy. When she got the blame, and I got the sympathy.) Intention was there to 'do better', recognising that the strength for this comes only from 'the Boss', which was my favourite name for God, and commitment. I made an unreserved submission to a Master whose love and trust was already well proven in my life. It was a natural step for me, but it was also a lifelong vow – the most important decision I have taken in my life, and one which I have never regretted. First, I trusted him with my life, then I literally 'stepped out in faith'.

It was early autumn, and there was no fire yet in the grate at my grandparents' house in Castle Avenue on the Antrim Road to the north side of Belfast. We visited it almost every Sunday evening after church, and I always looked forward to Auntie Rae's sandwiches. (She still makes more deliciously interesting sandwiches than I have tasted anywhere in my travels.)

It was a big house, with plenty of room for their six daughters and one son, my father. To me, as an eight-year-old, it seemed huge, in comparison with our three-bedroom semi-detached. However, it was the fireplace that became etched for ever in my memory. My height as an adult is 4 feet 6 inches, but as you can imagine at eight I was a great deal smaller. The fireplace was big enough for me to walk right into the hearth, if I only could – walk, that is.

'Well,' said Grandpa, 'what are you going to be when you grow up, Hilary?' Grandpa, a mechanical engineer, tutored at the Technical College, and always carried wonderful things in his pockets – silver paper, bits of string, old nails, scrap metal, all sorts of rubbish. He could make something out of just about anything, and my dad was the same. If you left coiled wire, cardboard, paper, tin, cotton wool lying around, then before you could say 'Lego', either man would have turned it into a miniature silver chalice or racing car, a crown or a sculpture, to place in the palm of my hand.

'What,' he repeated, fiddling with a ball of string which he had taken out of his pocket, 'are you going to be?' I told him about my commitment to Christ. Then I confided, 'God wants me to be a missionary.'

At the age of eight, I assumed that missionaries fought lions and tigers in the jungle – Africa, India, China were in my imagination. I'm not sure that Belfast was in the running; it was much later that my homeland as a missionfield became a much more pertinent calling to me.

'Ah,' said my grandfather, the renowned McDowell sense of humour twinkling in his eyes, 'that's good. But Hilary, I've never seen a missionary being pushed through the African bush in a pram before. Wouldn't the wheels get stuck in the undergrowth?'

I thought about those wheels. I had seen no wheelchairs for children in those days, and I was still being pushed in a lightweight, deckchair-shaped pram known as a 'tansad'. For the first time, I really thought about the practicalities of my lack of mobility. He was right, it would be a bit difficult.

'God's going to make me walk,' I said. 'Yes,' said Grandpa, 'but when, Hilary?' 'I don't know,' I admitted. 'When he says so.' Grandpa smiled, and began to unwind the ball of string. He stretched it across the open fireplace and attached it to either side.

Smiling again, he pointed to the string. 'What are you waiting for, why not now?' Watching him stretch that string slowly across the chasm of the hearth, I realised God had been waiting to answer the eight years of prayer – but that I had to take the first step. Thanks to years of faithful petition and exercising from elders, schoolteachers, minister, family, and friends, I stood to my feet, held on to that flimsy piece of string, and walked across the fireplace, the full width of the hearth.

REPLY FROM A LIVING FOETUS

Three weeks, they said,
Three weeks at best
Was life expectancy for her,
Who'd ask for more?
For a foetus damaged accidentally, irretrievably.
Some phase within the womb aborted
But not the seed itself.
The doctor said,
It was like nature waging a battle to evict
And losing –
He wasn't sure who'd won.

Forceps were the midwife.
They bit hard against the broken face,
Jaw shattered in as many pieces
As a splintered dream.
One ear only hearing,
One eye squint.
She'll never walk, they said,
She'll never speak.
Lower limbs disjointed, dislocated,
The mother simply asked,
'What'll I do?'
They said,
'Take her home.'

Eight years we prayed—
Father, Mother, me.
Mum and Dad, I don't remember hearing in that time
One regret expressed,
Not one regret that love had brought me here.
I learnt from you that nothing born of love
Makes misery,
And no architect on earth,
Or any other sphere,
Goes to his lathe
Without a draughtsman's plan.
And God, if architect and father both he is,
Will not feed his children with a stone
Or when he's asked for fish, serve up a serpent.

I aborted death—
When at the age of eight
Accepted Yahweh, maker of the Jews.
He brought his son to me
And in gentle, spiritual, intimacy
The one whose name is Jesus took my broken parts
And proved to me that not one piece
Had been abused.
I walked that year.
Doctors can't say how,
I only know
It was his touch that made me whole.

And here I am,
To show a daughter's love,
Offered to the world
Tentatively in shaking hands,
Holding out forgiveness in marked
And resurrected palms.

3 'YOU MUST GATHER IT YOURSELF'

Some folk remember little of childhood. I am blessed (and cursed) with extensive and vivid pre-adolescent memories, providing almost total recall of many childhood experiences.

On the blessing side of the equation is the memory of our annual harvest visits to Mr Davidson's farm in the rich apple orchards of County Armagh. He was a cousin by marriage on my mother's side of the family.

I recall him as a big, quiet farmer, with little to say yet much to communicate. His open arms did the talking and his eyes. My impression of him was one of overwhelming generosity. We returned home after every visit laden down with all kinds of fruit.

On arrival, he would be standing at the open doorway, big and unkempt and silent, flanked by two labradors: one black, one golden. My dad would carry me to greet him, and I would be asked the same question every year, 'What'll you sing in church this Harvest Sunday, Hilary?' 'All is safely gathered in,' I'd reply. 'Then how can a city child sing this, unless she's helped to pick the harvest herself?'

He would reach for the baskets, and out we would go with him, the whole family and myself, to the masses of apple, plum, and damson trees to reap the harvest – my sister Dorothy running on ahead and climbing trees, and eating the fruit faster than she could gather it. One year, seeing the amount of damsons she had consumed in one go, I announced that tomorrow, in church, she would be a 'damson in distress' if she ate any more. Thereafter, this became ensconced in the family quotes. Daddy had to carry me, as the long grass between the trees was too rough for me even when I began to walk. Sheena, the black labrador, stayed at our feet. Each time we visited, it was her nose that welcomed me even before I got out of the car. This dog could carry eggs in her mouth without cracking the shells, and often her master demonstrated her intelligence with this and many other tricks.

On one of these visits, Mr Davidson was waiting for us out on the main road before we were in sight of the lane that was his driveway. He waved the car to a standstill, and hunkered down beside me as I opened the back door, my eyes searching for the black labrador. The dog was nowhere to be seen. The farmer, now crouched at eye level to my own, asked his usual question:

'What will you sing this Harvest Sunday, Hilary?'

'All is safely gathered in,' I replied.

'Then, Hilary,' he said, lifting his fingers to his mouth and giving the familiar whistle to Sheena, 'you must gather it yourself.'

From the garden behind raced the black labrador, and on its back bounced a little harness and reins – complete with cushion and seat. Sheena was to be my steed. Today, I would not pull the fruit off the branches from the lofty position of being perched on my father's shoulders. On this occasion, the branches had come down to my level. As I moved to the driveway, I could not believe my eyes. All along both sides of the smooth tarmac were branches of fruit trees stuck into the ground. Mr Davidson had severed them from the trees, and planted them at the level from which I could gather my own fruit while riding on Sheena's back.

The Queen of Sheba could not have felt more regal than I did that day. The dog kept stopping every few steps to look back at me to see if I was all right. Even if the cushion on her back moved ever so slightly, she would turn her head and wait for instructions. I have never felt safer, and I was doing it by myself. Never will I forget the feel of the dog's soft fur; the tug of the fruit from the branches; the scratch of the basket against my legs; the brushing of the leaves against my face, as I stretched beyond my reach, and found my reach longer than I had ever believed possible.

Many years later, when faced with the decision to launch out into full-time service for the Lord, arguments came from every side. People engaged in much debate regarding my becoming a 'missionary', and many outside the family circle voiced extremely practical concerns to attempt to dissuade me. And what did God do? He played before my mind the picture of that day at Mr Davidson's farm. In glorious technicolour, I saw again the two labradors, Sheena and the golden dog. Saw Mr Davidson at the open door, felt Sheena's strong fur beneath my palms, her warm body under me. Saw her head turn to check if I was all right. Felt the cushion slipping, but not falling. Remembered the joy in my parents' eyes. Daddy stepping aside, confident of my ability to cope.

Above all, I felt again the smooth texture of the fruit as it came away ripe in my hand. Smelt it fall into the basket. Heard the words, and whether they were Mr Davidson's or God's was hard to tell. 'You can't sing the hymn, "All is safely gathered in", Hilary, unless you've helped to gather it yourself.'

God does not give someone a job to do without providing the necessary tools and equipment to do it. 'I don't know how I'll do it, Lord,' I said, 'but here I am, send me.'

THE CALL

Eight years old and called to the ministry,
Eight years old and not a day more,
Go now, Lord, let me start right now
I have love to give, I have perfume to pour,
Wait, my child,
There's no hurry, my love,
Your feet tread on an icy floor.
There's a crying and aching and hurting to do
There's a dying to do, and more.
Go now, Lord, let me go right now
To the sea where the fishes are caught,
I will swim and dive and fight the waves
Till the nets to the shore are brought.

Wait, my child, there is time still
For the water's plunge,
There is time for the spray and the surf,
For the spume, and the rocks, and the whale's tooth,
To measure and prove your worth.
Let me love you first, my little one,
Let me love, and caress, and hold,
For there's times to come
In the bitter storms
When you'll lift your arms to the cold.

Let me come now, let me come, Lord,
Now that the dying is here.
Let me rest in your arms
And lie in your love
Till I feel your hope vanquish fear.
Come now, my child, for now's the time,
Now's the time when I'm here.

4 'DON'T WALK, FLY'

God's greatest gifts to me were Christian parents. Looking back, I know that if Mum hadn't sweated blood over my leg games and the discipline of the tedious journey to the hospital and back every day without a car, I might never have realised that legs were meant for action. Without the long-distance stamina of my mum's efforts, I would never have walked. Without my dad, I would never have learnt how to fly.

He was a poet. Not by profession, for he earned his living as an electrical contractor. It was a one-man business that brought in small amounts of money erratically.

His capacity for work was inexhaustible, but it was his spiritual energy that taught me how to fly. His was the vision that stretched beyond the parameters of this planet; his the poetry, art, song, not to mention the imagination, that cherishes the commonplace, while at the same time lifting it resolutely to the summits of the spectacular. Before I could walk, he would throw me above his head and catch me, calling, 'Fly, Hilary, fly.'

On his shoulders I saw the world. His world of birds and flowers and plants. His world of delicately textured rocks and clinging plankton. His tactile world of soil running through the fingers, and of bees held gently between palms without stinging. The smell of crushed leaves dank underfoot and the clean dirt of farmyard creatures. Dad taught me that fear was not something of which to be afraid, unless I allowed it to become my master. I had one master, Christ. I need accept no other.

Wherever we went, my place was astride Daddy's shoulders. Despite being a tiny person, I viewed the earth from a great height. As I grew older and heavier, I had to be careful about the wishes I voiced, because I only had to look up at a craggy mountain, speculating in admiration 'I wonder what it's like at the top?', and before I had finished the sentence, he would have me on his shoulders and be striding towards the foothills. Believe me, that man would never stop till he gently lowered me on to the topmost rock to admire the view from the summit. A big man and strong, a first-class runner and sportsman in his student days, but nevertheless the perspiration on his forehead often used to make it slippery for my hands to hold on to his head as we lurched and slid and stumbled to the top.

He never once let me fall – not even when we crossed the notorious Carrickareed rope bridge in County Antrim. I looked down and saw the water crashing against the rocks hundreds of feet beneath us. He was stepping very slowly from rope to rope, both his hands gripping the side twists so hard that they left red streaks across his palms. With knees that hardly bend, my legs stuck straight out on either side of his neck. Without his hands holding on to my legs, only my own grip clinging to his head and neck held me secure. I looked down again at the flimsy tapestry of holes below us and to the sides; it bore little resemblance to any bridge I had ever seen before. It rocked like a boat to one side, and then to the other, and every few seconds it lurched sickeningly in the wind.

In my ears, I could hear my mum anxiously calling for us to turn back. On the firm ground at the other side of the bridge, I could see strong, able-bodied tourists with hiking packs on their backs, and stout climbing boots, shaking their heads – and obviously having second thoughts about the return journey over the bridge which now oscillated like a swing.

We were almost half-way across. The wind had risen. I said a wee prayer out loud and then, with eyes still shut, turned my head in glee to the smell of surf and glorious storm-sting in the face. Daddy stopped and whispered, 'Well, Hilary, what do you think? Will we turn back or go on?'

With the wind and the spray and the motion and the pungent tang of the sea on my lips, I was flying already. 'Go on, Daddy,' I yelled at the top of my voice. 'Go on to the end.' He did, and with God's grace, so will I.

FOR JAMES McDOWELL

He could have been a farmer—
The way earth moved through his fingers as he spoke,
Instead his thumbs pinched lengths of cable into twists
To shove behind the skirting boards
That owner-occupiers might have light.
But then light was his business,
Whether it came from wall circuits, or the Bible,
His was the power to make it flame.
Enthroned upon his shoulders I viewed the sunset
From hills that should have been beyond our reach,
Summits the strongest athlete
Would count the cost to climb.
Frightened, as I grew, to name the goal
Lest carrying me to his grave I'd attain it.

Farmer, poet, father,
Planting your private sonnets
In the soil as far as our garden gate
To give me courage to stagger on beyond the fence,
Reaping where I had not sown,
Perhaps that's why it's me now
Ploughing a furrow across your grave
With my pen.

> Jesus said, 'No-one who puts his
> hand to the plough and looks
> back is fit for the Kingdom of
> heaven.'
>
> [Luke 9.62]

5 THE DAY OF
LOST THINGS

Auntie Ellie has been like a second mum to me. Living alone, just a short distance down the road from us, she was to be found more often in our house than her own. We were her family as she never married. She lavished all the love that was hers to give on both Dorothy and myself. She is not one to have an inflated estimation of her intellect or skills, yet this woman is a real prayer giant. With a singularly Ulster sense of humour, she used to say, 'God will be tired listening to me' or 'He'll be sayin', "It's not *her* again, is it!"' For if ever the edict of Paul to 'pray and pray without ceasing' was obeyed by anyone, it is obeyed by Auntie Ellie.

Every exam, every dread or anxiety, every spot or strain, or wrinkle of our brows was instantly transferred by her directly to the foot of the cross. She bombarded heaven with a constant barrage of requests on behalf of others, and her faithfulness and consistency in this ministry went a long way to sustaining my strength, even at its lowest ebb.

Always willingly available as a babysitter, she would count Christmas cards with us on the mantelpiece at the festive season, and invent games that involved us trying to guess which card the other person was thinking of by giving each other clues – using its contents of snow, or robins, or whatever. Auntie Ellie would push my pram on long walks along what we all called 'our wee road'. It led up the 'Mountain Loney'* where the buildings gave way to the foothills of the Black Mountain, and a pure stream ran fresh from its source and poured into our picnic cup from the rock fall. Nothing

* 'Loney' – an Ulster word for small lane.

tasted fresher. Or we would go to the Bleach Green where, at the height of the Northern Ireland linen industry, the cloths had been laid out on the field to dry. This 'wet bleaching' procedure produced the famous linen whiteness, which was not the original colour of the fibres. Redundant in modern times, the nearby dam – which had once produced water power for the mill – now provided a welcome haven for the odd fisherman who wasn't too particular about what he caught.

On the day when Auntie Ellie and I visited the Bleach Green with my lovely dolly, a fisherman was there, unsuspectingly casting his net into the water and only half-noticing the child further along the bank in a tansad. I was a great stone thrower – well, I thought I was. Many's the time Daddy and I had skimmed pebbles off the rocks and into the sea, counting how many times we could make them jump the waves. This was a pond, though, with no waves, but I was not about to miss an opportunity of interaction with water – which was, after all, my favourite pastime. In my right hand, I held dolly, and in my left, I clutched the stone. Unfortunately, I was right handed, not left, and when excitement and automatic pilot took over, the raised arm was right instead of left, and the emphatic lunge towards the water projected the doll flying at breakneck speed into the dam.

Auntie Ellie tells me that the scream I emitted would have awakened the dead. The fisherman did not take time to glance around. In he plunged, Wellington boots and all, to rescue, as he thought the falling child that must surely have made the splash and ear-splitting scream he had just heard. Emerging from that bleach green, with I can't imagine how many years of silt and muck dripping from him, his face was a picture. He stared at the doll now clutched in his hands as though he expected it to speak, and I did not understand at the time why my aunt and he should double in two with laughter. As far as I was concerned, he was a hero, and my doll was saved. Maybe it helped to instil in me a faith in human nature, after all not

even the Bible suggests that we should risk our lives for a doll!
Thus my sense of humour was born early, and so also was the
belief that lost things, and people, are never quite beyond the
finding.

Later, I discovered that Jesus had the same idea when he
said: 'For the Son of Man is come to seek and to save that
which was lost' (Luke 19.10) and . . . 'him that cometh to me
I will in no wise cast out' (John 6.37).

Ever since I can remember, lost inanimate objects have
been the bane of my life, and contribute greatly to my earthly
frustrations. Thankfully, God, as always, teaches me – even
through my habit of misplacing things.

THIS IS THE DAY OF LOST THINGS

Ready now to leave the house
With the briefcase neatly packed,
The files, the lunch, the Kleenex,
Skilfully stapled, wrapped, and stacked,
I've made all preparation,
Checked that everything is there,
One more thing before I go
I decide to comb my hair.

I've made sure the cooker's off,
All the windows tightly shut,
The sockets are unplugged,
And I've just to lift my coat.
The clock is looking friendly
And I've taken every care
But just before I go, I know,
I'm going to comb that hair.

It isn't in the handbag,
It isn't on the shelf,
Not in any of the drawers.
Perhaps it's in the plastic bag
I used for shopping yesterday—
No, that's in the bin.
Now surely somewhere in the house
I've got another comb.

I search and find;
The drawers are full of rubbish,
And the bin's been emptied now.
The shoes are in a heap below the bed
Instead of neatly in a row.
My search unearths lost coins and pens,
A few cobwebs I'd rather not have found,
But still no comb.

Now I'm racing round in circles,
Don't know where I'm coming from,
All I really need to do
Is just to find my comb.
Right now, breathing deeply,
Thinking tranquil thoughts—
It can't be very far away
Perhaps it's in the car.

Measured steps upon the driveway,
Fully in control
Of body, mind, and soul,
Garage entered,
Breathing normal,
Counting one, two, three,
Hand upon the car, oh no—
Where's the key?

It isn't in the handbag
Nor pocket of the coat,
It might have fallen underneath the car,
Pity my knees don't bend,
Never mind, on stomach now,
To search that dirty concrete ground
From end to oil-streaked end—
And still no key.

Get the spare from bedroom drawer,
Stairs to climb
And out again in record time.
Driving to the meeting now
Knuckles white upon the wheel,
Traffic's heavy, but I'll only be a little late,
Soldiers searching on the bridges!
Traffic stops – for a forty-minute wait.

I think a bit,
And pray a bit,
And all those little things I should have done,
And could have done,
And would have done,
If only there'd been time,
Ghost-like come to haunt me
As I sit, deadlocked, in line.

And like a bright balloon
Whose air has all escaped
Flattened, I ask the Maker if he's given up control,
Of every neutral thing that doesn't have a soul.
And he puts a thought into my head
To challenge and remind,
'This is the day of lost things, Hilary,
'For all of humankind.'

The day of lost things – lost things, Lord?
You mean we shouldn't get upset
With tyres that sweat, or tubes that leak,
Or computer disks that sweat?
For we're not lost,
Lord, you know exactly where we are.
On your map, my situation,
Is not located in this car.

Steadied now, becalmed of mind, I think,
Before I can forget,
I must write that down,
I reach forward to the dashboard then
To let my fingers do the walking,
Then laughter lets the tension fly
As the realisation dawns—
I can't find my pen.

6 'IF I COULDN'T BE ME'

Daddy introduced me to my closest friend – the closest one on earth, that is. I am not sure exactly when it happened; I cannot fully remember the day or hour, but, for as long as I can remember, Dad and I were both seriously in love with the sea. It is hard for me to imagine that some people stand before the ocean and see only water. For me, song is there and music; God's whispered chorale of shouted glory. I can sit for hours in its company, harmonising my soul with the sound and the scent and the touch and the pain of it. There is no peace elsewhere for me as can be found in contemplation of its depths, and its moods, and its changes. No pain like the joyful pain its beauty brings. No pleasure like the scent of its pungent smell. Knowing the sea, I sometimes wonder if anyone would ever need any other lover.

An avid reader and writer even before primary-school days, this is the earliest poem of which I still have a copy:

IF I COULDN'T BE ME

If I couldn't be me
I'd rather be the sea.
If I couldn't be the sea
I'd rather be a tree.
If I couldn't be a tree
There's nothing else
I'd rather be.
I'll just be me.

Such an early-developed sense of self-worth is rare, and perhaps likely to be more so in circumstances of disability, but all human beings, disabled and able-bodied, long for love that is unconditional. In my work of Christian counselling, I know that much (if not all) of the anger, depression, and hurt feelings presented by ordinary people are rooted, to some extent, in a lack of self-worth and the inner need for unconditional love. Unfortunately, we cannot experience such love upon earth.

However ideal the care and devotion of parents and others, from our earliest years every child experiences conditions – 'If you pass your exam, you can have a bicycle', or 'Sit still in church and I'll give you a sweetie' – and the conditions become more subtle and complex as we grow older.

Unknowingly, the loving parent 'programmes' their offspring to expect love, praise, and affirmation to be conditional. The human infant, albeit subconsciously, develops believing that it has to 'deserve' to be loved. It must somehow prove itself worthy to merit the positive attention. If parents/ teachers have been over-critical of the child in its early years and it experiences a lack of progress at school, then the negatives are being reinforced, and the infant is likely to develop a poor understanding of its own abilities.

The good news is that we do not have to be stuck with this image. It *can* change. Awareness of the situation and the psychological path we have walked since birth, often traced back to and including the birth experience itself, can reveal traumatic memories which, when brought under the healing power of God, can be transformed to a bedrock of new and positive foundations towards a concept of our self-image.

In the light of God's unconditional love for each one of us, we can discover the true 'image of God' which he has placed within every human being, and which each of us chooses either to affirm or deface, as we choose to accept or reject him who loves us, without conditions.

In my youth, and still today, whenever I need solace or

peace I make straight for the sea; and thankfully, my family has never lived far away from water. Belfast, a city surrounded on all sides by green hills, is also within easy distance of the sea – less than half-an-hour's drive in any direction will get me to water of some description. From my bedroom window where we lived at that time, in Springdale Gardens, off the Springfield Road, I had a lovely view of the Black Mountain and, if I tilted my head a little, I could just catch a glimpse of the dam behind the hedge and fence at the top of our cul-de-sac. It wasn't sea, but it *was* water – and that 'tided me over' until the end of each week when we could have our Saturday run to Carrick or Bangor. Further afield were the famous Mountains of Mourne at Newcastle or the wild Atlantic ocean at Portrush, or just about anywhere I fancied on the Emerald Isle. I had only to take the notion, and we would be off 120 miles to Dublin itself. If it was possible, we went. If it wasn't Daddy made it possible, and we still went.

With the hindsight of adulthood, I marvel at the extensive journeys my sister and I enjoyed in our childhood. Dad's one-man electrical contracting business kept him very busy, but as far as procuring customers was concerned, it was either a feast or a famine. Often, when things were busy, he would literally have to work around the clock to complete the assignments. He often sung Mum's praises for the way she handled the budget. Even today, she can still stretch a pound further than anyone I know!

7 'JUST TAKE WHAT YOU CAN'T REPLACE'

Perhaps I learnt early that happiness bears little correlation to wealth. My late teens and early twenties were dominated with the practical implications of what we in Northern Ireland affectionately call 'the troubles'.

Still living at that time on the Springfield Road, my sister and I suddenly faced early curfews, imposed mainly by our parents' anxiety. A previously quiet residential mixed area, housing families from both sides of the political divide, it lies between the Shankill and the Falls. Extending as it does from the foothills of the Black Mountain to the centre of Belfast town, it was considered to nestle precariously between 'a rock and a hard place'.

Either end there was no other way out except through one or other block of almost exclusively segregated housing areas 'orange' or 'green'. If the exit at its town end through the Grosvenor Road was blocked, any one of the three alternative routes took the traveller through areas of potential flashpoint. Even the Grosvenor Road itself provided little in the way of security, squeezed as it was between the adjoining Shankill and Falls, as all three roads moved closer together on their approach to the city centre. At times of street rioting, when barricades sprang up with such speed and geographical unpredictability that we felt as if we were constantly walking on marbles, social life came to an abrupt standstill for days, and sometimes weeks, at a time. Our home was permanently prepared for a state of siege. The house occasionally served as the fortress from which we did not stray, except to go to work or attend church.

Then the burnings started. We heard it one morning on the

news: 'Protestant families burned out of their homes in the Lower Springfield area'. We lived further up the Springfield Road in the mixed middle-class area, but I had friends living only a few minutes' walk down the road in Merkland Street and Cuppa Street, where many folk lost their homes by fire, or by squatters moving in to take over whilst they were out shopping.

The 'troubles', until then a nebulous fear that generated avoidance strategies, suddenly came home to roost. No longer confined to staccato bulletins on the news, which were compulsive listening even for the young – if only to know which roads to avoid on the way home that night. The fear became dramatically located on our own road, and threatened to proceed, literally, to our doorstep.

As time passed the attacks intensified, and street by street was burnt; the plague creeping up the road towards us, house by house. It was well known that the perpetrators were not from the area itself. Gangs of strangers would invade areas where folk were living peaceably together, and set fire to houses belonging to adherents of their 'opposite' politics. This took place in both Protestant and Catholic areas, with each set of alien hoodlums as bad as the other. From both denominations of religious affiliation people found themselves homeless, or so afraid of attack that they moved away before it happened. The vans and cars trailing little mounds of salvaged furniture passed the foot of our cul-da-sac, and each day their number increased as families sought refuge within housing estates that were almost exclusively one 'sort' or the other. Belfast was slowly, relentlessly, being segregated – not by choice, but by fear.

Terror builds slowly and stays long. Each trailer passing jerks another twinge to the heart. Each pungent suggestion of smoke in the air induces another tensing of the muscles. Every newstime impels an obsessive switching on of the radio.

But it was the small domestic stresses which were the most telling. Our routine of family life did not change, but the faces of my parents became tense: the times when they moved to the front of the house to look out of the window increased; Daddy was talking in strained undertones to Mum each time he left or returned; Mum kept checking and rechecking the locks on the doors. New and stronger locks were fitted, but neither my sister nor I needed to be told that those locks would be totally useless against a flaming torch or a homemade battering ram. Yet the human psyche has an immeasurable ability to push such things to the outer fringes of consciousness. I did not *feel* I was living on a knife's edge. I was aware of the danger and took care in travelling, but I daresay there was, to some extent, a sense of denial of the circumstances. Whether I was blinded by this, or whether it was due to my continuing trust in God to keep us safe (perhaps a combination of both), I fervently believed it would not happen to us.

It was after 11.00 p.m., and I was asleep in bed, the night they came. Daddy wakened me by gently shaking my shoulders. His face, bending close to my good ear, seemed unperturbed – even smiling a little so as not to frighten me.

'Get up, Hilary,' he said softly, 'we have to pack.'

My feet were on the ground before I was properly awake. 'What's wrong, Daddy?'

He raised the blind a little, and pulled back the net curtains of the window beside my bedhead. 'They're on their way up the road, love. Maybe they won't come this far, but I think you should put a few things in here.' He tapped my tiny vanity case underneath the dressing-table. I kept bits of jewellery and memorabilia in it, and the case was small enough to balance in the open palm and fingers of my hand.

Daddy's eyes were a mixture of tension and tenderness, but the strain was evident. He put his hand on mine as I stretched to open a drawer in my dressing-table. 'Just take what you can't replace, Hilary – nothing else.'

He left the room to tell my sister. There was no time to count money in my purse, so I did not reach for it. No time even to select which of my many translations of the bible to take – I knew I could buy them again. Instead, I unlocked my vanity case and up-ended it on to the carpet.

There, in an undiscriminating heap, lay my precious things: half-a-dozen pieces of jewellery, all presents from my loved ones on birthdays and Christmases past; curled photographs of my heart-throb Cliff Richard, holiday snaps of my family and friends; a small handwritten notebook of my poems, scribbled since I was very young; valuable coins Dad had once collected from all over the world and then given to me as a token of where I would one day travel; other bits and pieces of teenage sentimentality, which were of significance only to me, but gathered from many years of an early developed sense of occasion and a 'making of memories'.

'Take what you can't replace,' he'd said. I grabbed the photograph of my family. It was one of all three generations together, including my deceased grandfather. The notebook of poems went next into the case, and other notebooks which I hastily grabbed from shoe boxes beneath my bed. I knew I would never be able to remember or write those thoughts again, not in the way a child writes. They were my testimony to a loving God and what he had done for me.

The tiny case was full by now. I lifted the small silver key to lock it, and as an afterthought grabbed one piece of jewellery. Not the one of greatest monetary value, but a delicate gold bracelet of open and closed hearts given to me on my last birthday by Daddy. He'd talked of his love for me, and how God's heart and his heart would always be open and loving me wherever Dad himself was, or whatever happened to either of us. I took time to lower the bracelet into the vanity case; it fell between the photo and the notebook of poems, and I could hear it rattle as I turned the key and lifted the handle on top to carry the case to safety.

It was an odd feeling standing at the door of my room, potentially saying goodbye to everything I had valued so far in life, holding those few items in my handheld vanity case. Clutching only love and creativity and hope. Standing there in nothing but my pyjamas and the dressing-gown I'd snatched from the inside of my bedroom door, my feet incongrously boasting my strongest shoes because there was no support for me in slippers. If I needed to run with the family in the dark night air, I knew I should wear stout shoes, to avoid falling and holding back their escape. I said goodbye. I looked around the room and out on to the landing, and I imagined it burning, all of it, every bit, and without trace. Maybe I was in shock, or maybe God had a hand in it – probably both – but I felt nothing. Only gladness that if I had to leave, it would be with those whom I loved. I prayed then, and kept on praying. That night I discovered, first-hand, what is irreplaceable.

Thank God, the terror did not come into our street that evening. The threat halted at the corner. There were no burnings that night on any part of the road, nor was Springdale Gardens ever again visited by such a group during our time there.

I like to think it was the joint witness of Catholic and Protestant living in solidarity in that street which turned away the unwelcome strangers that night. I know that my father would have had no time for threat or counter-threat, for he lived his life as a witness to the non-violent strength and love of the living Lord. That night, the lions' dens came to us, and God did not ask my family to walk inside.

He did, however, ask me to take a good look at what I valued in life, and to adjust my priorities.

TAKE ONLY WHAT YOU CAN'T REPLACE

Wardrobe of vanity
Hung with pride,
Step away
Or step inside the
Coffin of death
Where the spirit dies,
Walk away
Where freedom lies.

Clothed only in memories
Sculptured in pain,
Feel the dark night
Embracing the rain,
See the sparks fall,
See bright horror fly
As burnt flakes trickle down
Watch your memories die.

Chase them not,
Let them go,
As unicorns dance
Where time is slow,
Grasp your chance,
Break shackles free,
Remove the mask
Let the naked eye see.

My family and I lived on in that house for several years after the onset of 'the troubles'. My parents eventually moved, but not until after Dorothy was married and I was a qualified deaconess, living away from home in a flat of my own close to my work.

Like all trouble spots around the world, the situation in my homeland is infinitely more complex than a few minutes' listening to the bulletins on the news can reveal. The anomalies and seeming contradictions of belief and practice of politics and religion never fail to astound me, and sometimes they can be both poignant and humorous in the telling. Contrary to popular 'foreign' belief, the inhabitants of Northern Ireland are not shooting each other behind every bush. It is possible to have lived here, in the Province, for twenty years and more and never to have seen anything of the violence first-hand. This is both a strength and weakness of the situation.

On the one hand, a person cannot live on a knife's edge

indefinitely without cracking, therefore a certain amount of emotional and psychological 'distancing' from the turmoil is applied unconsciously by a great number of people in the country. This is necessary for them to continue to operate on a practical level, in a situation where something might or might not happen, but most probably will *not* happen – at least, not to them. On the other hand, detachment must never become callousness, nor must denial become apathy. There is no danger of that, though, in the worst affected areas. It can be said that those who have suffered most and are closest to the victimisation are the ones who are often, but not always, the most forgiving.

It is also indicative of the inhabitants of Ulster – with our 'thrawin'* nature and inborn ability both to laugh at ourselves and, at the same time, tolerate seemingly crazy contradictions of politic and practice – that common reactions to the most everyday events are capable of producing situations of black humour. For instance, many a time in the course of my work I have witnessed folk from both communities willingly 'give their eye teeth', as we say here, to help their 'opposite number' who, having found themselves in a 'bit of bother', are glad to accept this help. Yet would either of these communities move a single inch in their hard-and-fast voting habits? 'Not a inch,' they will tell you – and boy, do they mean it! Such contradictions gave birth to the following poem.

* 'Thrawin' – pronounced 'thran' – is an old Scottish word used in rural areas of Ulster to mean extremely headstrong and stubborn.

EVER GET THE FEELIN', BOYS?

Do you ever get the feelin', boys
That nothin' quite makes sense,
And if Christ would preach his mountain speech
This land would call him dense.
Yet insult the cross of crucifix
And they'd nail you to a tree,
For there's never been a man on earth
More blind than he who will not see.

Do you remember the day when auld Sadie's cat
Climbed the garden wall,
With barbed wire caught under both its feet
All scratched and cut and screechin' hard
Till you couldn't hear yourself speak,
      Or think,
      Or pray,
      Or wash the yard.
And auld Michael Rooney just out of confession,
Grabbed hold of Sadie's orange window dressin',
And rescued the brute with a swipe of his hand,
Though the scratches he got were bleedin' grand.
Right through the day it bled and bled
And Sadie gives thanks that the cat's not dead,
And often hopes that God'll bless Michael's head,
And goes on to hatin' R.C.s she's not met instead.
For she thinks he's not bad, though he is what he is,
But the learnin' is old, like she learnt it in school
And to her he's the exception that proves every rule.

>And do you ever get the feelin' boys,
>Ever get the feelin' boys,
>Ever get the . . .
>Boys a-dear-a do.*

Lily's lived on the Shankill mostly all of her life,
She's never been a criminal, she's never been a wife.
Remember the days when week after week
She trapsed† to and fro next door,
With a drop of soup and a friendly smile
To Theresa's niece
With the baby born of a marriage mixed and broken now,
And Lily likes to do what her heart can allow,
For the girl's too young to be hated yet,
Lily thinks she's not bad, just terrible sad
Though she's one of those, and Lily doesn't suppose
She'll ever be any different now.
And Theresa thinks the auld soul's a dear,
And a pity she's proddin' the grave with her foot,
For the country could do with more of here here.
And she'd like Lily to stand for the wee 'uns big day,
But the learnin' is old, like she learnt it in school
And to her, Lily's the exception that proves every rule.

>And do you ever get the feelin' boys,
>Ever get the feelin' boys,
>Ever get the . . .
>Boys a-dear-a do!

* An Ulster expression of poignant exasperation.
† Ulster word meaning a combination of 'tramped/hiked/struggled'.

8 ECHOES OF THE CALL

I could not ignore God's nudgings. Every morning in the early 1970s, I awakened with the memory of God's challenge to me at the age of eight. The challenge to serve him in some kind of missionary endeavour. My last thought every night before falling asleep was, 'Yes, Lord, send me.' If I could have ignored all this, I might well still be working in the Royal Victoria Hospital, Belfast, or in my subsequent position as private secretary to the registrar at the Belfast Royal Academy, one of Northern Ireland's top grammar schools. What great memories I have of both places, and the good friends I made in each of them.

But, for me, these duties kept me too far removed from the 'coal face' itself. God was leading me to the front line in his will for restored wholeness of body, mind, and soul for all. The call was clear; the motivation was strong. By the mid-1970s, I knew the time was ripe, but so many questions still remained unanswered. Where *is* the missionfield? How can I serve there? What about the physical considerations? God had long since disposed of the pram whose wheels might stick in the undergrowth, but I was not exactly running the minute-mile. My limit was 100 yards walking distance maximum before total exhaustion set in.

Were these my thoughts! No, I confess they were not. However kindly the advice was expressed, these were nevertheless the deliberations received from all and sundry around me, outside the family circle. I knew what they meant though. They meant me to recognise my limitations and, to put it bluntly, 'wise up'.

The aspect of limitations, however, has not seemed to

figure too largely in God's considerations when choosing people to serve him in the past. Biblically speaking, the boy Samuel, young David, Gideon with the greatly reduced army, Moses with the inadequacy of speech, Peter with the blundering mistakes, Mary of Magdala with the immoral past, inexperienced Timothy, and Paul with the thorn in the flesh, to name but a few, all said an unreserved 'Yes' to the call of God – and they were not turned down. As a matter of fact, Paul's insistence that '[God's] strength is made perfect in weakness' (2 Corinthians 12.9) is because of God's sufficient grace, and not due to any ability on our part. This theme repeats itself most forcefully throughout the Bible, in both Old and New Testaments, at the specific points of greatest inadequacy in the lives of those attempting to obey God's call to service. Paul himself was strongest when at his lowest ebb: 'I know both how to be abased, and I know how to abound: everywhere and in all things I am instructed both to be full and to be hungry, both to abound and to suffer need. I can do all things through Christ which strengtheneth me' (Philippians 4.12–13).

Although I cannot claim to be in Paul's league, we do have a thorn in the flesh in common – one or two – and if it worked for him . . . well, it's the same God, isn't it? The same God who brought an insecure Peter walking across the water to the boat. Who took the fear of death from the heart of Moses and equipped him to face the awesome terror of the massed armies of Pharaoh. The same one who stopped Paul in his tracks, and turned a zealous Pharisee into a lion prepared to face a den of Daniels and make himself one with them.

When all the arguments were argued, and all the logical, rational, objective wisdom voiced (and the list was as long as my arm itself of the reasons for not proceeding into full-time service) I ran to my dad for the last word. He just smiled, and – in that gesture that I'd seen him use a million times when there were no more words to be spoken – lifted his hand upwards and pointed towards the sky. On that day, I knew nothing would stop me becoming a missionary, because it wasn't me they had to stop. That evening in church our new minister, the Reverend Harold Gray, preached about being called into full-time service. The coincidental nature of the subject-matter stunned me – but then, I daresay that organising a little coincidence is a slender task indeed for a Boss who is accustomed to parting the Red Sea.

I don't remember the details of the sermon, but I know Mr Gray dwelt for a long time upon the call to one particular person, someone of the twentieth century who had not believed they could have served God, yet God had equipped them. I have a feeling it was a member of the royal household, but I'm not certain. My mind was whirling at the timing of the subject-matter itself – it made a deep impression, coming as it did during my time of fervent prayers for guidance on the subject. At the end of his sermon, Mr Gray challenged the congregation by saying, 'Perhaps there is someone here tonight who feels God is calling them to consider full-time service for him?' When my minister wrote those words in his sermon preparation, I wonder if he ever expected to hear a knock on his door shortly afterwards, and on opening it to find a 4 foot 6 inch leprechaun answering the call.

It is a measure of the stature of the man that, in our subsequent chats together, he never so much as blinked in embarrassment or reservation at the practical difficulties I might encounter, but gave me great support and encouragement to proceed step by step with all the necessary enquiries towards God's calling. I was also encouraged by Sam McClintock, who was a young assistant in Woodvale at that time.

There was one more 'fleece' to put before the Lord before I took the final step of making formal application for candidature as a deaconess. Like Gideon, who literally laid out a fleece on the ground and asked for it to be sometimes wet and sometimes dry as confirmation of the Lord's will, I tried my own version. Not so much a fleece, as the taking of a high risk.

I asked Mr Gray to pray for me as I went on holiday alone to the Channel Islands. Sounds easy enough, doesn't it? But I had never been away from home before without the support of either family, friends, or my faithful blue invalid car. My maximum walking distance was 100 yards at a time and with the many physical handicaps, plus different climate, different food, increased walking, pressure of the journey, I knew that anything could happen.

Livingstone striding towards darkest Africa could not have experienced more trepidation nor excitement than I felt as Daddy waved me goodbye on the quay. Mum was crying, and I heard Daddy whisper to her, 'You've got to lose your children to keep them, Betty.' He too felt the anxiety for my safety just as keenly as she did, but he also recognised the prerequisites to flight. Unless the parents are prepared to nudge the chicks out of the nest, wings never stretch, feathers never spread, no one gets airborne. Daddy was in the business of seeing me fly.

Jersey is not exactly the far reaches of the Orient. Its lifestyle and customs are very British and familiar. But, to me, it was the physical adventure of my life, and I was alone – except for the Boss, of course!

There was, however, no one but myself to carry my far-too-heavy case. I was alone on my own two feet, not having negotiated with the taxi-driving populace before (thankfully they showed me nothing but courtesy and kindness); independently attempting my extremely weak and rusty schoolgirl French in the European restaurants, and alone as I lay down to sleep in a strange hotel out of reach or call of anyone I knew or trusted.

'Show me,' I prayed, 'show me, Lord, that it is all true, that you can make all things possible.' Oh yes, I knew he had called me to be a missionary, and thanks to him there were no wheels now to get stuck in the undergrowth, but there were still skinny legs that would not bend properly, internal organs that didn't obey the Queensbury Rules, and a host of other physical problems and inadequacies that I was determined would not get in the way of my 'deaconessing'. I felt at that time that if I couldn't manage the work physically, I had better discover this before I took the step towards a life vocation in the diaconate ministry.

I would like to be able to tell you that I never fell down on the pavement on that holiday, that I never stumbled along with the perspiration soaking my clothes in agony with the effort of walking beyond my limits. I would like not to mention the times I ended up in a crumpled heap on the grass with heart and lungs bursting through my chest with sheer exhaustion. I'd like to say that my case didn't feel like the workload of a chain gang, and that I never felt the panic of the darkness, or being lost, or feeling embarrassed in company at the unexpected idiosyncrasies of a body suddenly plunged into circumstances beyond its remit. I'd like to, but I can't, because at times, it was sheer torture. More than once I wondered, 'Whose idea was this?' But then the Boss and I would laugh together; and he would chuckle in the way he frequently does with me, and put into my mind the thought, 'Well, nobody said it was going to be easy, did they?'

Easy, it was not! Yet by the end of the holiday, I knew it was possible. With 110 per cent effort from me, and the extra 500 per cent from God, it was not only possible, but confirmed.

It was especially so on the day I bought a return ticket on the hydrofoil across the narrow channel of water to St Malo in France. They told me it was the shortest trip to the Continent – however they did not tell me that it is also frequently the roughest. That day even the cabin crew were green around the gills. On every side of me people were being violently ill. The smell was awful. The craft rode up beyond each oncoming wave, and slapped down with a mighty crash on to its crest, only to be carried along with a rolling surge to the next rollercoaster. An avid sailor all my life, I was enjoying the motion of the boat but beside me, a young French mum was almost oblivious to the baby in her arms, and the toddler clinging desperately to her skirt. The standing infant was unnaturally quiet with fear, and the newborn babe was, thankfully, fast asleep. The young mother rocked back and forward moaning softly to herself, her hands and hair soaked with perspiration, her face even more ashen than the humid, overcast sky.

She turned to me blindly – I doubt if she even saw me – and with a nauseated voice droned, 'We're going to drown.' She spoke excellent English, and we had already exchanged casual greetings before setting sail. 'No, we're not,' I reassured her. She grabbed hold of the lapel of my coat with one hand, real terror in her eyes, pleading 'How do you know?' I took her free hand in mine. 'I know,' I said slowly, 'because God is with us and I have work to do yet for him.' 'Can you guarantee?' she asked, her voice high-pitched by now, and approaching hysteria.

The cabin crew were moving towards us to assist her. 'Promise me,' she yelled, 'promise me we're not going to drown.' 'I promise,' I whispered, 'trust God, trust him.' She thrust her baby into my arms, and the toddler automatically transferred its grip from her skirt to my knee. It clung to me limpet-like without making a sound. She turned towards the cabin stewardess and was violently sick. Afterwards, I stroked her head and mopped her face clean with one hand, while the baby slept silently on my lap, cradled against my other arm. The toddler stood like a little Trojan, contented with a fleeting smile and a wink, and the odd tickle from me every now and then throughout the journey.

It was, as I said, a short crossing, but the young mum swore that she would never sail again. 'I'll fly,' she said, 'I'll only fly from now on.' 'So will I,' I thought, but I wasn't thinking of aeroplanes. God had confirmed yet again that he never gives a person a task to do without supplying the tools necessary for the job. He can use us despite, and often because of, our inadequacies. I returned home, and applied to be considered as a candidate for deaconess training.

I never saw that young mum again, but she and her family

often figure in my prayers. I know they arrived home safely, because she sent me a lovely thank-you letter with a beautiful silk scarf which I treasure, and I fully appreciated her trust in me that day. For that's what the kernel of living is all about, isn't it? It is trust, not ability or confidence or talent, but trust. It is having faith in the midst of the 'not knowing' that pays dividends. It is the going forward in trust, whatever the outcome, that proves faith's greatest hopes.

I was very much reminded of this requirement to believe in the right outcome regardless of the odds when, in the autumn of 1993, Northern Ireland suffered the terrible 'trick or treat' massacre. A group of loyalist paramilitaries entered a pub at Halloween and shot many of the customers, calling 'trick or treat' as they did so. Much 'tit for tat' retaliation was taking place at the time and continued afterwards, with many innocent people suffering from both sides of the divide. I wrote the following poem.

NOT KNOWING

Trying to sleep on Halloween night
Not knowing if the loud reports
Are shots or fireworks.
A child squeals in the darkened street outside,
I listen,
Not knowing if she squeals with delight, or terror.
I pull the blind up just a little, squinting through,
Pulse racing, mind praying,
Not knowing if I'll see Catherine-wheels or blood
Upon the street.
Three tiny masked figures are knocking on the door
Across the way, chanting,
'Christmas is coming, and the goose is getting fat,
Who'll put a penny in the old man's hat.'
The street is quiet except for them,
The stillness is dark except for them,
The future is black—
Except for them.

No one else opens their door
To the children's high-pitched voices.
All fear that if they did,
Then behind the little ones, up the driveway
Might come a taller figure wearing a balaclava
And chanting 'trick or treat'.
There is no knowing.
It is the not knowing
That bears the horror of this Halloween night.

Paul shipwrecked,
Struggling up the beach,
Bitten by the snake,
Not knowing if the poison
Would be his death call.
Paul languishing in prison in Rome,
Writing letters, singing praises,
Not knowing if anyone would read his words.

Peter walking into the darkness
From a fireside betrayal of the Lord,
Not knowing as his master dies
Whether he himself would ever be forgiven.

John on Patmos imprisoned until his death
Writing visions of tomorrow,
Not knowing if his shorthand
Codes of warning
Would reach the churches' ears.
There is no knowing.
Only faith to keep believing,
Walking, writing, hoping.
And oh, my friends,
Look what came of love,
Look what came of it—
In God's time.

9 THE MISSIONFIELD

At the time of my application for full-time service in the Home Mission of the Presbyterian Church in Ireland, the legislation to admit women to the ordained ministry was only just beginning its lengthy process through the courts of the General Assembly. The channel for service that was open then was as a commissioned deaconess. Later, when ordination was an option for women, I still felt called to the lay ministry. My yearning to be at the 'coal face' included a fervent desire to be an enabler. To help every member of God's community, ordained and lay, to take their place fully in ministry to the body of Christ. I felt then, and still feel now, that I can best fulfil this task by remaining a member of the laity myself. If I ever change my mind, it will be because God changes it for me – I do not intend to change it for myself. As for me I will continue to 'serve the Lord; for he is our God' (Joshua 24.18).

Growing up in Woodvale Presbyterian, a deaconess to me meant one thing only – Winnie. Winnie Shaw had laboured long and untiringly in my home congregation throughout my growing years. Hers had been the constant visits to our home; hers the familiar face popping up in Christian Endeavour meetings, and in Sunday School and Girls' Brigade, and just about everywhere else, it seemed to me then. She extended friendship when, as a child, I accepted her kind invitations to keep her company on her regular rounds of visiting the elderly during the long summer school break when I would otherwise have had little to occupy my time.

I will never forget standing clasping the flowers my mum had picked from our garden in my perspiring hands, waiting beside Winnie, half-excited, half-terrified, on some stranger's doorstep, wondering what on earth to say when the lady of the house opened the door, and the hours quietly listening to the chat. Winnie's cheerful, compassionate tones reassuring the frail; her touch reaching for the bereaved hand; her unashamed retort to those in need of rebuke; her quiet tears shared with the hurting. Long before I had any idea that the deaconess ministry was to be mine, God was training and teaching me through his experienced servant. She did not know it at the time, but her generosity of openness and sharing was paying dividends for me. Thank you, Winnie, and thanks for still being my friend all these years later.

Now that I am in what is officially known as the 'middle years' (although I would not dare to call myself middle-aged, as I feel I am just about ready to begin my schooling now), I would love to be able to revisit the date when my application to be considered as a deaconess candidate for training in St Colm's College, Edinburgh, was received in Church House in Belfast. How I would now love to be a 'fly on the wall', as the committee opened that letter and read its contents. Much debate must have taken place about the practicalities, for the deaconess ministry is nothing if not physically exacting. Apparently, they had no qualms about my ability to cope with the extreme mental, emotional, and spiritual stress of the work, but I know they did falter at the thoughts of the physical demands: the endless corridors to be walked in the regular hospital visiting; the flights of stairs in the twenty-storey flats to be climbed (especially when the lifts are not working – and that's in the blocks which have lifts at all); the tramping in rain and snow during the door-to-door visitations; the controlling of the members of the youth club and the camps and sports, and the effervescent toddlers in the crèche. The list of the extreme physical requirements of the vocation is endless. But vocation it is, and I thank God that the selection committee, led by Miss Margaret Nicol, applied great vision to the subject and exercised their natural insight and understanding within the situation.

Many years later, I heard of some of the heart-searching with which those faithful servants of God wrestled over the period of the several interviews with myself. Lives and examples from the past bore silent testimony to God's enabling power to make all things possible; and I believe one committee member even quoted Gladys Aylward, whose frail health and diminutive stature had resulted in one church missionary society of her day turning down her application to go to the missionfield in China. Using her own finances, Gladys travelled 'freelance' to China – and, as they say, the rest is history. God himself gave her the strength to cross hostile terrain in China's bitter winter conditions, helping many orphaned children to flee the advancing enemy troops across mountain ranges to her Inn of the Sixth Happiness and safety. I did not know that I was to owe Gladys a favour on the day at the final interview, when I was called into the solemnity of the ancient stone walls of the Assembly Buildings, Church House, headquarters of the Presbyterian Church in Ireland. I sat there shivering, more from nerves than from the temperature in the corridor.

I tried to imagine life the following day if they said no, and tried to imagine an alternative. I could not – life beyond that final interview was a blank. I could see nothing, imagine nothing, want nothing, except what would happen as a result of an unconditional 'yes'. I have never stood in the condemned cell awaiting the call to walk the corridor towards the hangman's noose, but I think I came very close to experiencing such feelings on that particular day. A 'no' from the committee would, to me, have been the sentence of the black cap. I would have gone on serving the Lord somehow, but right then I could not imagine how.

Knowing what an outright 'no' would have done to me that day, God, in his graciousness, spared me from it. However, he had much to teach me about patience, and I did not return home with an unconditional 'yes'. The interviewing panel explained the need to pass my medical, and how they believed I might fail it. I tried to interrupt; I tried to ask them to send me for a medical examination anyway. I tried to explain what I knew from God's walk with me thus far: that, with him, all things really are possible. I wanted to go straight there and then and face an examination for the crucial medical certificate. God, I believed, would have me pass it, whatever the odds.

But they were not about to be deflected from their decision. Instead they offered me an ultimatum. Would I be prepared to leave my position with the Belfast Royal Academy and do a year's pre-training, full time in a parish, with no guarantee that I would finally be accepted as a candidate? It was, in fact, a physical endurance test in place of the statutory medical examination. I said 'yes' without hesitation. I realised it was going to take a little longer, but I was at last on the right road.

The parish they chose was one of the hilliest, most difficult walking terrains in Belfast, for Eglinton Presbyterian Church was situated under the shadow of the Black Mountain close to the Cave Hill on the north side of Belfast. Many of the streets in the vicinity rise sharply, at a gradient so steep that often articulated lorries would jacknife in their effort to negotiate the slopes in bad weather conditions. In fact, during that period I remember there being a number of serious accidents of this type.

At that time, the Benview/Silverstream estates, rising to the steep hairpin-bend road known as 'The Horseshoe', boasted a number of high-rise flats – without the luxury of working lifts. In addition to this physically challenging terrain, the area was undergoing in the early 1970s the same 'burning-out' and relocating victimisation of sectarian violence that I knew only too well from my own neighbourhood.

The Ballysillan Road had originally been a mixed area with good relationships, but the sectarianism of the recent years was quickly turning the estates on the slopes into Protestant ghettos, and the worst casualties of this trend were the mixed marriages – of which Eglinton had quite a few. However, the congregation had two great positives going for it: generous and warm-hearted people, and a saint of a minister. The Reverend W. D. Boyd rarely spoke without a smile in his voice. His affirming laughter rang out through every day's struggle in that place. He it was who taught me the value of recognising the might of God and the integrity of his calling, while, at the same time not falling prey to the temptation of taking oneself too seriously.

I was to begin on New Year's Day, Monday 1st January 1973. On New Year's Eve, I went to the Watchnight Service at Eglinton, so keen to get started that I could not begin soon enough. W.D. gave me a great welcome, as did the congregation, but when at 1.00 a.m., on leaving the service, I asked if I should report for duty the next morning at 9.00 a.m., W.D. threw back his head in an unrestrained guffaw. 'What!' he grinned, 'I'm going home to my bed, and don't you get out of yours till the sleep's left your eyes, Hilary. If you turn up at the Manse before 10 o'clock, you'll have to start without me.'

W.D. and I were quite an experience for each other, and in all my time at Eglinton I never once saw him out of sorts, yet I knew full well the weight of responsibility which lay upon his shoulders, and how the events of those troubled years must have torn him and his gentle wife apart on the inside. Yet his sense of humour was never quelled, nor did he withhold his time from those in need. The staff meetings in the Manse on Monday mornings were the highlight of each week for me, and were marked by much prayer and hilarity. This gift of genuine accessibility to people is a hallmark of his successful ministry, and the foundation of the deep affection by which he is held in the memory of all who have had reason to come to him for help.

The first time he asked me to preach from the pulpit, I tried to decline the invitation. My hesitancy was not due to lack of experience – thanks to a lifelong membership of the Christian

Endeavour (C.E.) movement, I had been given much enjoy-
able practice since early childhood in speaking and leading in
the Junior C.E., and participating later in the youth and adult
sections. My home church had one of the strongest C.E.
groups in the Province. It met every week, and there a large
number of future ministers and missionaries were nurtured in
the faith, and trained to take their place in full-time service
for God both at home and abroad. In addition to this training,
both my home-church ministers, Mr Craig and Mr Gray, had
provided me with many opportunities to speak in public
throughout my school years. But there I was: not yet trained at
St Colm's, no theological qualifications to date, no badge, no
uniform, no title. I felt a bit of a fraud for the first and last time
in my life. The feeling lasted about two seconds – just long
enough for Mr Boyd to ask me, with a big wink, 'Haven't you
got something to say to these people, Hilary?'

That sentence has travelled by my side all the way down the
years ever since. In the worst of times, it has spurred me on
whenever I felt the weight of my own inadequacies. I knew
then that what I had to say was more important than any of my
qualms, or fears, or inadequacies, or pride. For what I had to
say was not my business, but the Lord's; not my message, but
his. When I stood for the first time in that pulpit, I was not
aware of how I looked, or how I sounded, or what anyone
listening might or might not be thinking. I could imagine only
one thing – Jesus – and with the thought of him in my mind, I
certainly did have something to say to the people. I've been
trying my best to say it ever since.

The months that followed trained me for my own personal
Olympics. January, February, and March of that year gifted us
with some of the deepest snow falls that I had seen since
childhood. Driving a three-wheeled invalid car is often a
freezing, deafening, lonely experience. But when it stops dead
at the foot of a 9:1 gradient, in snow that comes well over your
boots, and you've got visits to do in the high-rise flats at the
top of the street, and it takes you twenty minutes to crawl on

all fours to the top, and the lifts aren't working, and your clothes are soaking wet, and your head is aching from the effort, and the dank stairways of the flats are stinking with the smell of urine from the excesses of some of the inhabitants' Saturday-night binge, and you've got to crawl up them on all fours because your bones are hurting too badly now and your back will not straighten, and you dare not wear gloves because you need a good grip so as not to slip from the snow on your boots, and the spittle on the stairway is now all over your hands before you reach the top and you ring the bell, breathless and demoralised, and no one answers the door, what then?

Well, I confess that I cried. Chiefly from exhaustion, but not for long. At the sound of steps ringing hollow on the uncarpeted stairway above me, I wiped my face with the clean lining of my jacket and smiled a sunny W.D. smile at the lady who stood, in tears, in front of me. 'Are you coming to visit *me?*' she sobbed incredulously. We went inside her flat, and she talked of standing on the roof of the high-rise block, of gazing down the steep hill feeling she had no reason left for living. Swamped by depression, she described seeing 'a wee critur'' crawling through the snow, and thinking, 'If *she* can keep on going, what am I doin' complainin'?' I had not exactly cast myself in the 'wee critur'' role; indeed, I had rather fancied myself becoming a respected deaconess one day. But God had an even bigger sense of humour than W.D., and he too wanted to make sure I didn't take myself too seriously. He also wanted to remind me that it is only by his strength that any achievement in the Christian life is possible.

Many a tear I have shed in my ministry since, but never again did I cry because of physical inadequacy in the course of attempting to minister to another. For, like Paul, I had learnt the secret God taught him also, 'My grace is sufficient for you, for my power is made perfect in weakness' (2 Corinthians 12.9).

IN CHARGE OF EMIGRATION

Which angel did God choose
To be in charge of emigration
On the day I was dispatched,
    New hatched,
    Mismatched,
    To planet earth?

When was it heaven lost
The written forms for transportation?
Did the papers get confused,
    Abused,
    Misused,
    Filed under pending?

For me, I could believe
That just beyond the solar system
Somewhere a planet's waiting,
    Computating,
    Calculating,
    Why I never came.

An earth that's been prepared
With atmosphere as liquid, swimming,
Limbs unsupported, fluid
    Towering,
    Willing,
    Stringless kites to fly.

Instead I landed 'thud',
Gravity my nanny, nurturing,
On the dirt, tightrope walking,
    Balking,
    Falling,
    Marbles underfoot.

Requesting transfer, God
To that other place without delay,
I'm quite sure you'll understand,
> Take things in hand,
> This other land,
> Is dovetailed to my needs.

What's that you're saying now?
Papers will be processed in due time?
Stand in line,
> Get in the queue,
> Back view?
> What's new!

So here I am,
Stuck behind an applicant from Calvary.
And how long have *you* been here, Sir,
> Biding time?
> *What?* Two thousand years,
> And more.

Well!
I can plainly see,
What this administration's
> Done for you,
> Can do
> For me.

10 DARKER THAN AFRICA

While at Eglinton I had the privilege – and, for me, great pleasure – of helping lead the young people. I had been at the youth club that Friday evening in early February, but had left, as usual, when some of the boys who also led the group offered to see me safely reverse my invalid car down the steeply ramped strip on to the busy main road before they locked up.

When Mr Boyd phoned later with the terrible news, I could not believe it. One of the youth club members did not reach home that night, but died on the street. He was gunned down by those who probably did not even know his name – it was enough for them that he was leaving a Protestant church youth club. He lay dying for the same reason that many others would die, and those from Roman Catholic areas as well – merely because he represented the 'opposite' tradition to the gunmen who that night went looking for a member of the 'other' community from across the sectarian divide. Three others were injured with him. Each side calls the others 'the other sort'.

The following week's programme at the youth club and Youth Fellowship needed no structuring, for the subject was chosen by the members themselves. Their question was, 'Why?' It was a question difficult to answer. I'm still trying.

LET ME DO SOMETHING

She climbed into the car
With the burst of petrol bombs in her ears,
And the image of a hundred soldiers on her mind.
      'Just to get out,' she thought,
      'Out, anywhere, somewhere quiet.'
Somewhere where the city lets its talons relax,
Where she could drop into silence,
Hear herself think,
Where God is.

The city limits welcomed her,
      'God, are you here? Where?
      People need you.
      Why don't you go where people need you?
      Back there, world of cities.
      Are you blind?'
God looked down at her then
With eyes,
Eyes that Jesus Christ had used,
Eyes that had looked from a cross,
Eyes that saw, everything.

She tried to pray,
But fresh memories of fear and mutilation
Burst on to her consciousness and the city terror clung.
    'Be everywhere, Lord,' she cried.
    'Be, hear, answer the city,
    Be where people love and hate,
    Kill and pray,
    Lord, this city has a thousand sisters—
    Don't close your ears,
    Are you deaf?'

God's listening was so intense, it hurt.
    'All right, Lord, so you can see,
    You hear,
    Then please do something
    Why don't you *do* something!'

Worlds have floated into eternity
While waiting for answers,
With the quietness born of despair, she waited,
The answer did not come, nothing.
Only stillness.
She left that place.

She climbed into the car—
Through the mirror she watched the countryside retreat,
The city engulfed her and the car, and God, willingly—
It was very hungry,
Its name was Belfast.
They passed waste ground where houses had been,
They passed broken windows and burnt-out shops,
Washing beat against walls
And smudged some of the chalk marks,
The slogans screamed bitterly at the car,
And God spoke, quietly.
  'I can see it,
  I hear it,
  Feel it,
  I care,
  You know I care,
  I have the answer to all this,
  The power to stop it,
  But the choice is yours,
  Give me yourself
  Let me do something!'

In the summer of that year, W.D. went on holiday as usual – however, this year he left me in charge. Now that really does require a sense of humour. 'What if somebody dies?' I pleaded before he left. 'Nonsense,' he replied, 'nobody ever dies in July!' In the first week, it happened and I was introduced the hard way to bereavement counselling. But then, is there an easy way?

With typical wit, W.D. met me on his return with the quip, 'What are you doing to my congregation?' It was then that he broke the wonderful news to me. Since I had survived the seven months from January to July, Church House had decided to accept me as a candidate for the deaconess ministry, and would not delay any longer. They were willing to send me for training to St Colm's College, Edinburgh, that same year – September 1973.

I made one more request to the selection committee: 'Please let me go for a medical?' 'What!' they exclaimed, 'surely you realise that all you have done in the past seven months has released you from the requirement of such a formality?' But I wanted to demonstrate, if only to myself, what I had known all along, that 'with God all things are possible'.

Sitting in the doctor's waiting-room, my file was sent for – the one where all those years ago a doctor had scribbled the word 'miracle', because he could find no scientific explanation for my being able to walk. The file was produced, and I was questioned while knees were prodded and pushed, and proverbial hoops were jumped through, and heads were shaken in amazement. The doctor listened to my testimony and my heartbeat, and took my blood pressure and heard my laughter; and finally, in exasperation at his own amazement, he underlined the word 'miracle' on the page again, and wrote me a full medical certificate – passed with flying colours. I resisted the temptation to say 'I told you so', remembering Paul's warning that we should boast only in the Lord, and I was only too grateful to have been given that pre-training experience at Eglinton.

Yet I was delighted that when I packed my case for St Colm's College, nothing was missing, not even the medical certificate. God, though, knew I would have to acquire a great deal more than can be carried in a case or weighed on human scales in order to serve him faithfully. There was a lot of luggage to lose, and I daresay there is a great deal more fruit of the Spirit still to grow before I can come anywhere near being ready to serve him in the Kingdom.

11 AWAY FROM HOME

In the lateness of a balmy September evening, my three-wheeled invalid car and I crawled into Princes Street, Edinburgh, after a 150-mile adventure involving one puncture, one detour (when I got temporarily lost), and a number of enforced stops to allow the overheated two-stroke engine to cool down.

'Hullrontebib' ('Bib' for short) was no mean vehicle. He had been my companion through riots, barricades, and pleasant picnics all over Ireland, but he was not built for a non-stop 150-mile trek from Stranraer to Edinburgh. I confess I was in a hurry to get there, having waited such a long time for this moment, and at last here it was – Princes Street.

Never will I forget the thrill of my first sight of the mile-long stretch of brightly lit shops, and the sensation of living out a fantasy when that fairytale castle came into view. It seemed to me to be a beacon of welcome as Bib and I struggled and backfired in a slow crawl along the last furlong towards my destination.

I was tired, very tired, and the sounds coming from my mechanical steed were not at all reassuring. Yet none of this could suppress my feeling of elation. I was absorbing happiness: admitting large doses of it into my being with every breath as I felt my tears cloud out the sight of Princes Street Gardens with its hanging illuminations; until I had to concentrate really hard to bring the scene into focus again. I couldn't take my hands off the throttle; I dare not stop. The vehicles all around were treating me to an 'ordeal by fire' as they introduced me the hard way to what the traffic in a real capital city is like. Edinburgh seemed to dwarf the city of Belfast. I could not stop, because I knew Bib would not start again if I halted now. Most of all, I knew I must not stop because I had come so far, and my heart was bursting with excitement and fulfilment, and the thoughts of would I, could I, really make it on this last stretch impelled me on. Like a jockey willing her steed over the final jump, I tensed every muscle in my body and bent low over the throttle. 'Please God,' I said, 'please get me there – please.' Then I imagined the laughter in heaven. 'Hilary,' I imagined the angels saying, 'who do you think has got you this far?'

Bib was loaded to the roof with luggage and books, and three more cases were being transported for me in another car carrying fellow students on their way to St Colm's. Fortunately, both cars were by now travelling the mile along Princes Street in convoy. By the time I turned into Hanover Street, I was freewheeling. The hill sloped steeply downwards all the way to a T-junction, which was less than one hundred yards from the bottom of Inverleith Terrace – where St Colm's awaited me.

Bib, most considerate of vehicles, had got me over the brow of the hill before stalling, but he was in no frame of mind to start again. There I was with no engine power, no petrol, and without the strength of a sparrow in either the car or me, freewheeling in style at speed down this beautiful wide street. On all sides, cars were pumping their horns in the darkness. Taxi drivers treated me to the most incredulous looks as I overtook them with a wave, giving Bib his head to make that last glorious jump over the final hurdle.

Just another hundred yards, just a wee bit more . . . just . . . come on, Bib, I encouraged, and then stopped dead. The hill had levelled out to the T-junction, and it was necessary to let him rattle and shudder to a halt for the sake of fellow travellers on the road. I pulled over to the pavement and the car and I stopped, right there, within 100 yards of the sight of what would be home for both of us for the next two years. One last corner stood between myself and my destination. The college was not yet in sight – I was there, and yet I wasn't; it was humiliating. All that effort, after what I felt had been a successful journey, not to mention the years of waiting, praying, and working for this day, only to find myself unceremoniously 'dumped' at the very last post by a clapped-out, rattled-through, jumped-up old . . . . Then I looked at him standing there in the warm darkness, expelling steam and clicking cryptic messages from his inners. A single trickle of condensation ran down the inside of his fly-ridden windscreen, and I couldn't bring myself to kick him. Poor old Bib, I thought, he has done his best. What more could anyone expect from a mini-sized blob of metal. 'I'll just have to make the last 100 yards on my own two feet.' I said it aloud, and suddenly it dawned on me – *on my own two feet!*

Hadn't I waited for this day since I was eight years of age? Hadn't God put me on my feet at that age and removed all wheels that might 'stick in the undergrowth'? Hadn't he got me here through many stages and struggles? Wasn't he now, at the last, delivering me to the door of St Colm's without any form of security whatsoever: no strength, no guarantees, no wheels. I was to put my faith in nothing but himself. I turned from the three-wheeled casualty to begin my walk, only to hear a cheerful call from behind me. It was the driver of the car carrying the other students bound for St Colm's that night. 'We will send someone to get you,' she shouted. They organised a rescue with the staff of the college, and I didn't have to walk after all – but I had got the message from the Boss.

Old Bib and I were hauled in under sufferance. It was not exactly the conquering hero entrance I might have wished to make; it was more like the submissive servant. Nevertheless, it was an appropriate start to a thorough training in Christian service. Jesus himself showed us by his example of washing his disciples' feet that pride has no place at the banquet (John 13.1–17).

As I struggled in the back door of the college and staggered straight to an extremely necessary toilet, I could hear the other students being formally welcomed and introduced at the front door. Then, with a red face, I made my apologies for all the trouble my unusual arrival had caused. I had reached St Colm's safely, and in the process had jettisoned one more piece of luggage: pride, or at least a tiny sliver of it. That particular piece of human luggage takes a considerable number of removal procedures throughout life for its complete demise. I believe death to be the last surgical operation which removes its root. I thank the Lord for a sense of humour. Of all his dextrous instruments for pride-pruning, humour is the most lenient, most often applied, and also the most enjoyable teaching aid of them all. Even the pupil enjoys the masterclass when humour is the instrument of admonition. The Boss never laughs *at* me, only *with* me, but his jokes are such instructive fun.

Speaking of a sense of humour, I certainly needed one in the next hectic and exhausting, but challenging and extremely stimulating, two years of theological training at college. It proved to be one of the most wonderful and most demanding periods of my life, and a whole book would not constitute enough space to tell of the experience or the people. Sufficient to say that during that time, the friendships made and training acquired have lasted me a lifetime.

The policy of the college was to provide a training both soundly theological and eminently practical. During my six terms, in addition to lectures and examinations within college, the students were assigned to local churches to assist the ministers in the wide range of parish duties.

During my first year, I had a great welcome as a student assistant in Oxgangs, and in the second year at St Bernard's – the one-time parish of the Reverend George Matheson, who wrote that great hymn 'O love that will not let me go'. Standing in the pulpit of this well-known churchman, who had written the hymn when his fiancée jilted him on learning that he was going blind, I wondered what he would have thought of a severely disabled female preaching to the descendants of his congregation.

As I climbed those worn steps and stood for the first time in his pulpit, I reached out my hand to prevent myself from falling, and closed my grip on the historic cushion upon which that ancient Bible still rests. Imagining Mr Matheson watching me, I felt as if I stood in an extremely welcoming space. Standing there, gazing down in gratitude at the ageing and smiling congregation, I thought of the blind preacher with the broken heart, and immediately felt at home. I am sure that the Reverend George Matheson would have approved.

As students, we also spent additional blocks of a week or so in a specialised, and often residential, practical situation. I remember my time in the Royal Edinburgh Hospital (and also in the Royal Infirmary) 'scrubbing up' with the doctors, and observing operations in the theatre – where some of the male divinity students from New College missed all the interesting parts by fainting at the first incision of the scalpel. It is not to our credit that, later that day, the 'ladies' took some delight in 'filling the men in' on what they had missed – using some pretty graphic detail.

We also spent a residential week at Dundee with the local social services unit, paying house calls on needy families in areas of severe deprivation, and learning to analyse case studies and to develop interviewing techniques for counselling.

Perhaps my most vivid memory of all the external work placements was during the week they sent me to Greenock Shipyard on the Clyde. Being a petite 4 foot 6 inches, it was no hardship to squeeze into the narrow confines of a submarine in the making, and what a privilege it was to meet the men who worked there. Some were old hands, whilst others looked like lads straight from school. Without their overalls to identify them, the youngest ones might even have passed for my boys in the youth club at home. I thanked God for the hundredth time for the training I'd gained at Eglinton.

As I visited in the shipyard and in hospitals, and also taught in the schools, God was confirming that my ministry was at the 'coal face' – all those places where people live and work. He was calling me not to a building, but to a people, a people of God of every denomination.

In the summer vacation between first and second years, I had the honour of being accepted by the English Speaking Union to travel to America for a special project, teaching in a summer camp each day, and at night working on a drug rehabilitation programme among heroin addicts.

These were just a few of the many component parts that combined to supplement my training at college. It would take a great deal of space to describe the many rich experiences of pain and humour that cement a foundation for every student's future memory album. This is another tale for another day, but whatever way I might choose to describe my time away from home, it was certainly not an anticlimax. I will always be grateful to both the staff and students who shared the experience with me, and their dedicated contribution to my 'memory album'. No better poetry could end this chapter than the famous hymn written by George Matheson himself.

O LOVE THAT WILT NOT LET ME GO

O Love that wilt not let me go,
I rest my weary soul in Thee;
I give Thee back the life I owe,
That in Thine ocean depths its flow
May richer, fuller be.

O Light that followest all my way.
I yield my flickering torch to Thee;
My heart restores its borrowed ray,
That in Thy sunshine's blaze its day
May brighter, fairer be.

Oh Joy that seekest me through pain,
I cannot close my heart to Thee;
I trace the rainbow through the rain,
And feel the promise is not vain,
That morn shall tearless be.

Oh Cross that liftest up my head,
I dare not ask to fly from Thee;
I lay in dust life's glory dead,
And from the ground there blossoms red,
Life that shall endless be.

George Matheson, 1842–1906

12 PAIN – MASTER OR SERVANT?

It is not possible in the space of this slim volume to write about the events of my life from the mid-1970s to the late 1980s. This time included milestones such as my commissioning in my first parish of Carnmoney, and subsequent position in the joint Presbyterian/Methodist church extension charge of Taughmonagh, during which time my father suffered a massive coronary and died in November 1978. However, I do intend to explore a subject upon which I am often questioned: the subject of pain.

Shortly after my father's death, my tooth began aching in bed one night. I had had toothaches before, there was little novelty in that, but this was one king-sized ache. The next day, a hastily arranged visit to the Royal Victoria Hospital, where my adult dental work had always been carried out, confirmed the worst. When I was much younger, I had been told that my wisdom teeth would never develop normally, as they were lying horizontally inside my gums. When they did decide to grow, it would be the great-grand-daddy of all problems, as they would then extend horizontally into one another. This process would result in them becoming trapped, and entangled in many nerve endings connected to the brain and those controlling facial and other muscles.

This would require a difficult and delicate operation under general anaesthetic. I was grateful that the surgeon in charge prepared me for the ordeal. When the day came to operate, I was aware that he would not know which nerves had to be disentangled until he opened up the gum. The night before the operation, I lay awake in the hospital bed wondering what nerve ends would be severed, and which muscles affected.

What effect would it have on my brain, my face, my speech, the central nervous system? I wondered not with clear thoughts, but with my head reeling in agony from the unremitting pain of the toothache. Soon, I wondered no more. The pain became so tortuous that it took over everything, until thought itself became impossible. I put aside the books I had been trying to study in vain; as a newly enrolled student with the Open University, I was studying for an honours degree in psychology to supplement the counselling skills already gained at college. However, study became totally impossible that evening. I lay for hours praying, not with words, but aching my pleas to God. Mid-way through the night, sheer exhaustion and pain brought me to tears. I remember the nurse, on hearing my sobs, being both amazed and angry, in a gentle manner, at me not calling her sooner. She did not realise that I was not in the habit of taking anything to stop pain, but tried to cope with it myself. I have a serious distrust of drugs or pills of any kind, and would accept them only, as they say in Belfast, 'if my head was hanging off' – metaphorically speaking, of course. This is not a policy I would necessarily recommend to everyone. However, in my own case, I struggle to avoid any substance that might reduce clarity of mind or whose long-term use might lead to addiction.

'I'll bring you a witch's brew,' she smiled, 'you will feel no pain then.' As that gentle and caring soul left to 'stir the cauldron', she did not guess how little I was reassured by the nickname of the medication. I drank the smoking green/blue liquid, and settled down to a night of continued agony. Not one wink of sleep did I get, as the 'spell' didn't even make me feel drowsy. It did, however, reawaken my sense of humour, and the Lord and I chuckled together at the very notion that earth's alchemy, medical or otherwise, should ever come before his divine healing. The next day, they had the greatest difficulty in knocking me out with anything. Everything proved futile: the pre-med had no effect, and only the anaesthetic in theatre itself broke through the pain barrier and allowed me to embrace unconsciousness.

Regaining consciousness was one of the most frightening experiences of my life. The sensation of fear before the realisation of why you are afraid brings real terror, yet even before thought brought its healing, rational process to bear, God calmed me with the warmth of his presence.

Thinking was what I desperately wanted to do. 'Can I think? *What* can I think? Am I *able* to think?' I had desperately feared in the previous wakeful night that some vital nerve to the brain would be severed, robbing me of memory, logic, or creativity. 'Remember,' I thought, 'Hilary, what can you *remember?*' My brain was still fuzzy from the anaesthetic and everything sounded too loud; the softest noises were now clanging like Big Ben in my ears. I was deafened by the quietest whisper. Everything around me was irritating and frightening, and I felt sick. I was too scared even to open my eyes. The pain was no longer in my gums, but an awful frustration and irritation was buzzing in my head. I could hear my mum's loving voice beside me, coaxing me to open my eyes, but I wanted none of it. Even her voice felt like a pneumatic drill through my brain. I desperately wanted to be alone. Through the open doorway of the one-bedded side ward, the sounds of the other patients going about their normal activities were like corncrakes screaming in my ears. The pain of the noise seemed more intolerable than the previous agony of the toothache. Through swollen lips I mumbled, 'Too loud.' I half-opened my eyes, and saw the nurse move to close the door. I tossed my head from side to side on the pillow to try to ease the pain. 'Why don't they go away,' I thought. 'Please God, I need to be alone, I need to think. I need to know if I *can* think. Please send them away. I need to do it alone,' I prayed.

I shut my eyes and closed everything out. I wanted to ask them, 'How am I?', but I was too frightened. In my mind's eye, I asked God instead. 'How am I?' I prayed. 'You tell me,' I imagined him saying. I struggled to draw the thread of my mind into a coherent sequence; it was an immense effort. For the first time in my life I had to make a conscious effort to initiate thought, and it was a strange experience. I hated it. I fought the hate, and I fought the barrier to thought. Desperately, I reached out, like a child drowning, to grasp anything, anything at all that I could bring to mind. I would have grasped a straw, but God provided a rock. From the dark corridor of nothingness, I began to silently recite the twenty-third psalm. I did not stop until it was complete; I missed no line, I paused on no phrase. I knew it; I remembered it. *I remembered!*

PSALM 23

The Lord is my shepherd; I shall not want.
He maketh me to lie down in green pastures;
He leadeth me beside the still waters.
He restoreth my soul;
He leadeth me in the paths of righteousness for
    his name's sake.
Yea, though I walk through the valley of the shadow of
    death,
I will fear no evil: for thou art with me;
Thy rod and thy staff they comfort me.
Thou preparest a table before me in the presence of mine
    enemies:
Thou anointest my head with oil; my cup runneth over.
Surely goodness and mercy shall follow me all the days
    of my life:
And I will dwell in the house of the Lord for ever.

With his great sense of humour, I knew God would say, 'I think that answers your question.' It did; I was well. *I was well!*

IN DAVID'S DEBT

Thank you, David—
Smallest of the tribe,
Scribbling, watching sheep,
Herding sheep,
Dipping sheep,
Searching for the strays.
Burying the wolf catch,
Scratching with the pen,
The itch that boredom irks,
The itch that never ends.

Thank you, David—
Little man, made king,
Master of the harp,
Fleeing Saul,
Dancing prayer,
Searching for a friend.
Hiding in the caves,
Nursing secret pain,
The grief named Jonathan,
The grief that never ends.

Thank you, David—
Lineage of a God.
Making highways straight
With melody,
With artistry.
Some day walk with me,
Share a poet's heart,
Your tears wash my pain.
Thank God for greatness thrust upon you,
I thank him for the *joy* that never ends.

13 THE OLD ADVERSARY IN THE MIRROR

Anyone who has ever undergone surgery will know that the day of release from hospital dawns with mixed feelings. On the one hand, there is a longing for home, familiar surroundings, loved ones, and freedom to kick off the enforced routine of hospitalisation. On the other hand, there is fear. How will I cope? Am I strong enough? Most of all, how will others treat me or react to my new situation? Physical weakness can swamp us when the supports of clinical professionalism are removed. Even family and friends can prove more of a hindrance than a help by misunderstanding our altered circumstances, or the extent to which recovery is not yet complete.

For me, it was wonderful to get back home but I had an old and formidable adversary to face in renewed combat: my mirror. You might think that someone who had no reason to be vain in the first place would feel no pain in further diminished attractiveness. However, it does not quite work that way.

I looked awful. No, that was an understatement. To me, I looked hideous. My face, swollen and raw with a mouth that could only partly open, had no movement on the left side. Even before the operation I was to some extent paralysed on that side of my face, but had, throughout childhood, managed to coax my crooked smile to make some attempt at balance – and at least I was able to feel my hand upon my face. Now, as well as nothing moving, all was numb on the same side as my deaf ear. The result, to me, was devastating, mainly because when I smiled, or attempted a smile, it would jerk badly south on one side only, ending in something akin to a grimace. I had never resembled an angel, but now I was inadvertently doing an excellent impersonation of a Halloween witch.

The first time I tried to be with children, I felt my heart break. Lifelong allies and always my closest friends, I longed for their company but for the first time in my life they ran away when they saw my desperate attempt to smile. Who could blame them? The realisation that I frightened those whom I most loved did more to reduce my confidence than any of the difficulties I have had to wrestle with before or since. Suddenly I no longer cared about the lack of beauty; I only wanted the little ones to stay. Week after week of loneliness and inner torment sent me night after night pleading prostrated on the floor to my Saviour. 'Please God,' I begged, 'please give me back the children. I don't need to be pretty, but please just give me back my smile, so they won't run away.'

One early morning I was reading Psalm 84.8–12:

O Lord God of hosts, hear my prayer;
give ear, O God of Jacob!
Behold our shield, O God;
look upon the face of thine anointed!
For a day in thy courts is better than a thousand elsewhere.
I would rather be a doorkeeper in the house of my God
    than dwell in the tents of wickedness.
For the Lord God is a sun and shield;
he bestows favour and honour.
No good thing does the Lord withhold from those who walk
    uprightly.
O Lord of hosts, blessed is
the man who trusts in thee!

'*No good thing does the Lord withhold*', I thought, what better thing to ask for than the return of your smile? I knew then that God would not withhold it from me; I also knew that the surgeon had explained how the nerves had been severed and other nerve ends damaged which controlled facial muscles, and that he could promise no improvement. Nevertheless I wasn't going to let the facts or medical diagnosis get in the way of my practical, proven experience of the Boss. 'With men this is impossible, but with God all things are possible' (Matthew 19.26).

That morning, I put down my Bible and lifted my hand mirror, placing it on the table in front of my face – the same mirror which bore the legend 'any complaints about this particular model should be referred directly to the maker'. That day, I renewed the unequal, but powerful, partnership of restoration with the Lord, this time in respect of my facial paralysis.

Before breakfast each morning, I would get up and dress one or two hours earlier than usual, depending on the agenda for the day. Then came over an hour of exercising my face and lips. I use the word 'exercising' loosely, as not only had no one suggested any exercises for me to use, but literally nothing moved. I sat before the mirror praying silently, and desperately willing my muscles to move. Forcing, trying, straining, praying, straining, and day after day, week after week, month after month . . . nothing.

During this period, I continued my normal schedule of work. Nothing ended, nothing was reduced. Everything continued, the dramatising, preaching, and teaching. If anything, the demand for counselling sessions increased, and nothing seemed diminished with the adults – but still the children kept running away, and my heart kept hurting, undetected by anyone but God.

It must have been a good seven months or more after the operation when, seated before my hand mirror at 5.30 a.m., I tried the same exercise that I had attempted countless times already. Suddenly my left cheek twitched. I was scared to put too much store by it at first – perhaps it's the early morning chill, I thought; maybe it's an involuntary isolated twitch. But my heart was beating to African bongo drums as I tried again to force a response from now numb and stiffened lips. This time, the left side of my mouth moved. It actually moved – only about a hair's breadth, but it *moved*! The joy, the sheer joy of it. I soaked my mirror in tears, and had to reach for a tissue to dry it. I might not have been great at smiling in those days, but I certainly could slobber. Day by day, I kept up the exercises.

Within the week, I was smiling – properly smiling. Admittedly, the smile was crooked and crazy, but then it always had been. However, it was now a definite, indisputable, friendly, child-embracing smile – and the little ones no longer ran away. Once again, they knew I loved them because they saw me smile.

SUFFER THE LITTLE CHILDREN
AND FORBID THEM NOT

Let them come,
Let the children come.
There are barriers enough
To their growing.
Let them come,
Open up your arms
And let them feel your warmth.
Like bees to the nectar
Smell the sweet scent of their embrace
For they too fear the
Burnt winds of singed desert
On their upturned faces.
Looking desperately in your eyes
For a glimpse of a loving God.
Has he touched you?
Do you carry his presence?
It's not yours to keep
Let the children come.

14 FOR THE NEXT GENERATION

Over these past twenty years as a commissioned deaconess, working within a predominantly youth leadership context, young people and I have explored a great number of issues together. I have been asked many searching questions about life and God. One teenager asked the question, what had life been like for me? I said that it has been like the Olympics, only harder and much more exciting. Maybe that's why I identify so much with the comments of St Paul because, thorns notwithstanding, what the two of us have in common is a metaphor of the sportsfield. Paul asks, 'Do you not know that in a race all the runners compete, but only one receives the prize? So run that you may attain it. Every athlete exercises self-control in all things. They do it to receive a perishable wreath but we an imperishable' (1 Corinthians 9.24–25). This assurance of something to be won and something to be lost provides the impetus to keep striving. The prize for which I strive is to one day hear my master say, 'Well done, good and faithful servant' (Matthew 25.21).

Passing on that Olympic torch to the next generation is a glorious thing. An experience of stamina and adrenalin, of exhaustion and joy. For the next generation I would pray that they will have the spiritual stamina to continue the race, and that they will engage God's strength to fight the battle against evil and every negative aspect which threatens to encroach upon their lives. These days young people are thrown early into the maelstrom of secular influences and have to learn to sink or swim against the tide of materialism, immorality and the increasing pressures of a power-hungry, status-laden, society.

When some of our loved ones are members of the younger generation, we long to be able to protect them from hurt and harm. Many parents have shared with me the desire to shield their children, almost to the extent of attempting to live their lives for them. We know that this is neither possible nor wise, but what we can do is to offer them an example, and the example must be our striving towards a Christ-centered life-style, however imperfectly executed.

Take heart, then, for the next generation. If they walk in the footsteps of the Master, they may stumble, but they will not fall. In my own family I have been blessed with the great gift of a nephew and a niece. Alan and Julie are now in their teens. Alan, most considerately, was born four days early, in time for me to hold him in my arms and bless him just before I left for my second term at St Colm's. When he was small, we made models together, lots of them, until the garage at Dorothy and John's house became so full that my sister had to take things in hand and throw the lot in the bin. Out they went: sci-fi other-worlds of papier-mâché and string, new inventions to solve this world's problems, and monsters from our imagination. All these creatures and planets ended up where moth and rust have their way, but not the memories of the long hours of laughter and fun making them together, and not the dreams.

Often, Alan and I would talk of God, for he wanted to know this person. God was Alan's friend too, and his questions were blunt and uncompromising as only a child's can be. He wanted the truth – and that's what he got, all of it. Sometimes his search for knowledge led to very challenging and most humorous quizzing – like the day in his toddling years when I was telling him the story of how St Patrick came to Ireland to bring the Christian gospel to these parts. Alan's face, framed with golden curls, was screwed into a puzzled expression. So I continued, 'You see, Alan, people in Ireland didn't know about Jesus then.' He frowned again and turned a transparent gaze to mine, 'But why didn't *you* tell them,

Auntie Hilary?' Yes, it was hilarious but the challenge has stayed with me ever since.

They say that St Patrick chased the snakes from Ireland. When I wrote the following poem for Alan, I longed to help remove the reptiles that the ancient saint had missed. Snakes of violence and hatred, of prejudice and fear. My Lord's teaching showed me that the implementation of forgiveness and love was not an optional extra for the Christian. But how could 'Paddy' (which is in Northern Ireland a nickname associated more with nationalist and Catholic citizens than with Protestant Ulstermen) ever be united in teamwork with his opposite number?

As I tried to express in the poem, only 'an appreciation of the Saviour' will bring both sides closer together, but it will take more than a mere 'appreciation'. Total commitment to Christ and obedience to his teaching is what heals in Ireland. Prisoner, ex-terrorist, those raised within ghetto areas of one community or the other, innocent victims who have suffered great loss – all these have been able to unite in a working relationship specifically when their lives have been surrendered to the Saviour who makes all people one and whose touch makes each person whole.

Thank you Alan, for your challenge to follow in St Patrick's footsteps and tell Ireland about Jesus. In the Province it is our only hope. Thankfully, it is our God-given hope.

FOR ALAN

Take the snakes away, Paddy
Let the people live
Take away the snakes, Paddy
And let the children give
An approximation of the lovin'—
Realisation of the joy,
Take the snakes away, Paddy
For my darlin' golden boy.

Can we work together, Paddy?
Can we be a team?
Workin' on the isle, Paddy
Opening up the dream,
An appreciation of the Saviour—
Re-commitment to the Lord,
Can we work together, Paddy?
In the Kingdom of the Word.

When he was five years of age, Alan's sister was born – and what a sister! Lungs fit for the Albert Hall, complexion a perfect cliché – peaches and cream. As I leant over her cot in the nursery of the hospital ward, with her eyes tight shut and her lungs screaming for her mother (who was not yet conscious), I knew she would make her presence felt in the world. Tossing her head from side to side, she lay frightened and hungry, not yet touched by a member of her family. Julie's screams pierced my very heart.

I spoke only her name: 'Julie.' I said it firmly. 'JULIE!' Immediately she stopped and opened her eyes, looking straight into mine as though she already knew her name. I held her in my arms, and there were no more tears. Now an attractive and intelligent teenager, Julie talks of becoming a writer.

Living in today's modern society with its many stresses, Christians can sometimes exhibit symptoms of 'learned helplessness'. They are tempted to feel unable to be anything but victims stranded in a state of reluctant acquiescence to the pressures and negative influences around them, believing they have little power to change their circumstances or environment. For them, I share an extract of the poem written for Julie as she grew, because I believe that we are called to take an offensive, not defensive, position in the spiritual battle against evil. This fight to which the Bible rallies us in Ephesians 6.10–18 is not a 'fisticuffs' of the physical body, but a spiritual struggle to live the Christian life against all the odds, and in an environment that resists his coming Kingdom. Whatever it is we can wield – a spatula in the kitchen, a ball on the sportsfield, a pen in our hands – Christ can use every ability and talent, great or small, as a weapon to fight the negatives expressed in our society and prepare the way for his Kingdom. Jesus once described Satan as 'the Prince of this world' (John 14.30), but God is still in control and we must not forget it.

We are not powerless in the face of accident or nature or the circumstances of life. In conjunction with God, we can take control of our lives and turn disaster to victory, despair to hope. History itself awaits his authorship, and our implementation of his instructions to follow in his example of love and sacrifice. For Julie and all those who want to make a difference in the world, I offer this poem.

FOR JULIE

Write well, my love
Your pen will barbed wire tear.
Like tissue paper
Stretched across the trumpet mouth
To rend the deadened air,
Of hatred and of pain.
For into history
We walk like babes again.

15 POEM OF HOPE

'Write a poem of hope for Northern Ireland' was the request from the Greek Orthodox Academy, situated on the island of Crete. That was how, in August 1989, I came to represent my country at a World Congress of Christian Art and Literature there, and had the privilege of seeing my poem hung in the Academy, along with works of art, sculpture, and poetry from many of the world's other trouble spots.

With apologies to Shakespeare, here is the poem:

NORTHERN IRELAND

The children of my land lie cradled
in the history of their own making.
Like Siamese twins bound head to toe
along a single spine.
His life and mine entwined,
two minds with one obsession.
Their single goal—
freedom from each other.

What death at birth, what hell is this?
To enter from one womb
united in frustration of each other's presence.
Eternally together and forever strangers,
never looking, never seeing,
never knowing when his tears
match the quintessence of my own.
What loneliness is this,
to feel the lifeblood common to us both
fuel our two hearts with a single rhythm.
Wishing his to stop and know
that should it stop
my life would also go.

They say we look alike, my twin and I.
What cruel circumstance can bless a mother
with beauty twice arranged in such a fashion
that neither babe can gaze
upon the other's face.
Surely it must rumour only be,
he cannot look like me, for if he did,
I dare not hate him so.

Is there no physician
skilled with gift of scalpel's artistry,
who can, with swift and painless carpentry,
sever this dank, dark shadow's leech from me?
And leave me still alive – alone.
Yet rumour still I hear,
about a man, well, 'not so much a man,
though once he was',
and now he's more a mirror,
shining sphere whose iridescent light
can circumvent the proportions of every space.
Even rooms where twinned hate stands
back to back and fears in pain
to see the other's face.

And even as my brain gave credence to the thought
I saw a man, well, 'not so much a man,
though once he was',
approach me and with outstretched hand
hold out to me, not a scalpel,
nor even tool of carpentry,
but piece of burnished glass
and standing still between my twin and me,
where both by him were seen,
he raised that instrument of lustre skywards
till its reflection filled the room,
and I could see his eyes reflected
and in its mirrored depths – saw mine as well
and one other face was there,
but whose it was I could not tell.
I only know it looked like me.
And seeing it I longed for solitude no more
for we were three.

At the end of the project, I discovered that Crete had bestowed upon me a terrible legacy. The doctors said it was probably a slipped disc; on the other hand, they could not be certain what caused the gnawing pain that felt like a knife-thrust at the bottom of my spine. It developed a few weeks after my return to Ireland and was perhaps the result of the fall that twisted my back and stomach as I fought to stay upright with an overbalancing trolley laden with my heavy suitcase at the airport. Doctors speculated that maybe it was aggravated by the soaring Greek temperatures, combined with cool fans that dangerously wafted draughts waist-high to a Hilary. Or perhaps torn tissue and muscles were not healed properly. Or it might have been something else entirely that no one could fathom. Whatever the cause, the pain was agony, and one of the several specialists whom I consulted in the following few years described the pain as being three times in intensity as the worst labour pains. Personally, I think he was a master of the art of understatement. After the torture of two years of constant, unremitting back pain, I reckon that giving birth would be child's-play (if you will pardon the pun). Unless, as they say on all the best TV programmes, you know different.

I cannot remember exactly how many appointments Mum and I sat through during that time. It seemed as though hardly a week passed without us counting, yet again, the clinical stripes upon another sterilised wall. We must have watched dozens of kiddies bouncing in the playpen at the crèche end of waiting-rooms, and heard a hundred toys get the 'I'll break you before I go home today or bust' treatment. My Mum inherited a few extra corns from her toes being in the way of invisible tricycle tracks, and I became an expert on the unique species of butterflies painted by hospital artists to cheer up the hour-long, two-hour-long, three-hour-long (and, in some cases, day-long) waits to see the latest consultant. I thank God for the faithful prayers of 'Dawnwatch', four dedicated housewives – Ann, Roseanne, Carol, and Phyllis – who have been my consistent voluntary prayer support team for more than a decade. They continue to bring my work and personal concerns before God. With their regular prayer support, and that of other folk further afield – like my County Donegal friends Mrs Maud Lamberton, Michael and Kathleen McKenna, Margaret and Alan Speers, and many others around Ireland, north and south – I was able to take each day as it came.

Meanwhile, life outside the hospital appointments shrunk to the basic essentials: eating, sleeping, and working. Nothing else was possible, as the pain sapped all surplus energy for its own malevolent, sacrificial gratification. Just to stay sane it was necessary to channel every energy I had to fighting the pain. Once only did I try a painkiller, but it proved useless. I understand that different people have differing thresholds for pain. But in my work as a counsellor I meet many who are in need of help to come off drugs, as a result of long-term addiction to painkillers. I decided, against all the various doctors' advice, to resort to my normal and previously tried-and-tested better judgement of a 'no pills, no drugs, no painkillers policy', relying upon prayer and trust. And then I realised that this time more was required. To merely resist the pain would result in a broken back as I was already pushing myself well beyond the limits of my walking capabilities. I could not deny this pain and go about my business. Each day, after a full day's work of ten to eighteen hours, I would have to crawl the last few yards from the garage to the back door on all fours: hair soaked in the rain, wrists and arms splattered to the elbows in mud and dirt from crawling, and from clinging on to walls, fences, steps, hedges, anything that would help me drag myself along. I desperately pushed myself beyond previously excessive limits of endurance. I tried to walk differently to shift the balance, and to distribute the weight from the worst affected side. I cut out all social engagements to save my strength for work. I did not reduce my work-load, though, despite the many hospital appointments. I took written work with me to the waiting-rooms, and was grateful never to fall behind on projects – and I prayed. How I prayed! But even I could see, as the months stretched to years, that I was fighting a real giant here. In tears one night before the Boss, I confronted my worst suspicions. 'Lord, I can't fight this one, it's too strong. Show me what to do.'

God's answer, as always, was too simple for mere humans to have concluded alone. 'Don't fight it, Hilary, *marry* it,' he said. This was a hard word for an independent lady. Me, who had never submitted to anything in all my days, who had sweated and struggled to stretch herself to snapping point, never giving in to any pain or handicap, or negative of any description. Me, who would rather draw her own blood than capitulate to any master but Christ, was being told by her Lord to 'marry the pain'. My tears turned to anger. 'No, Lord,' I shouted, 'no, we can beat it, you and me, please Lord, work with me, we can do it together.'

Suddenly, in my mind's eye, I was in a garden. There were plants all around, and I saw Jesus kneeling beneath an olive tree. His back was towards me and he was crying; I realised it was Gethsemane. Turning from the sight, I shook off the image from my mind. I recalled his words without needing to hear them again: 'Father, thy will, not mine, be done.' I imagined myself lying beside the sleeping disciples, ignoring his pain for a few furtive moments of ease. That night, I cried properly; that night, I married the pain, accepting the union but not the bondage.

Jesus joined the pain and me. He never asked me to kneel to it in resignation, nor to be submissive to the evil of its restrictions, but to admit it to the flow of his love in me that it might never again be a tyrant, but might serve the growing of my soul. Instead of lifting my sword above my head and attacking it as it bore down upon me, I stood straight, erect in its path, and opened my arms to its advances. Once beside me, I placed it beneath my feet, and used it as a stepping stone to ford the wildest rivers still to be crossed. Pain, I learned that day, is only our enemy when we have not learnt how to make it our servant rather than our master.

MASTER OR SERVANT?

Partner or enemy,
Ally or foe,
Either way the guts retch,
The head opens to dark caverns of fear,
The self shrinks to the sum of its parts,
All else is gone.
When the hurting is with you
Nothing remains,
Only the pain.
Only the—
Nothing—
The only . . .
Pain.

Like breath to body,
Blood through capillaries,
It is the essential
Nothing remains.
Nothing else,
But the pain.

Then is the choice
Servant or master—
Which will it be?
False god of agony?
Bow the knee to that which is not Christ?
Servant be, I charge you
Ache and thrust, you will not gouge
Twisted submission from my soul.
Even though my face bears all the stamp
Of your dictates.
My spirit marries you
And in that union lies not still,
But fights and conquers till,
I your master will become.
For though I marry you
Never will you have a wife in me,
Not your husband either
But your master I am now,
And conquered by God's grace
You'll be a slave to me.

16 FREE AGAIN

Two years' pain partnered me; dark years and friendless with only work to distract my mind. Then, one summer, our General Assembly held its week-long business meetings in Dublin. As always, I enjoyed driving the two-and-a-half-hour journey south from Belfast, and quickly settled into the Bed-and-Breakfast where many other Presbyterians were staying for the duration of the meetings. It was a good week in June, and I had by now perfected the art of 'walking on walls' by putting all my weight on my hands and arms as they lent heavily on walls, street furniture, interior design artefacts, friendly passing dogs and their accompanying lamp-posts – anything and everything that came within reach to keep myself mobile, despite the continuing agony.

Open spaces were my dread, and I would sometimes stand for twenty minutes or more gazing at a wide open space praying for a car to drive into it and park, or a lady to abandon a shopping trolley in the middle of it, or a tall dog to stop and sniff a discarded sweet paper at its centre. Anything, anyone, just to let me have an oasis to dash towards and lean on to break the pain of the journey. I made a lot of canine friends that year, and became an expert on the relative strengths of the backs of the variety of breeds – not to mention their esoteric leg-lifting habits. By God's grace, I never seemed to be in danger of being bitten. Strangely, they seemed to sense my need of them, and most of the dogs helped willingly. I daresay that God encounters less frustration in moving animals to attend his will than humans! Maybe humans adopt more concerns to distract them from the gentle whistle of his signal.

Sticks as an aid to walking have always been more of a hindrance than a help to me, and I have never employed one. Besides, to ask me to use a stick is similar to suggesting to Jimmy Savile that if he got tired, he might consider finishing the London Marathon on a moped. Someday, I may have no choice in this matter and then I will graciously accept a stick or whatever else is necessary to keep me mobile. Until then, I pray that I can keep going under my own steam with God's help.

It was the Thursday of the week of the General Assembly. The day before had been particularly harrowing for me from a pain perspective, and that old partner had attempted to demand the upper hand. I had not capitulated, but I was exhausted nevertheless.

The afternoon took the form of a 'private session', where confidential matters of a judicial nature were brought before the Assembly. As a deaconess, I have chosen to belong to the lay ministry and, as only ordained members are admitted to this session, it gave me the chance to relax in the restaurant area with colleagues and friends. A table of ladies were enjoying a cup of tea together; and, as I reached for a chair to join them, the metal rungs of my seat slipped on the highly polished floor, and my bottom met the uncarpeted ground with a nauseating thud. Falling, never an alien experience for me, suddenly became terrifying. Like a fragile twig in the path of charging elephants, I felt my entire spine shudder as I twisted to attempt to save myself, and then felt my back jar on impact. Whether it cracked or not, I could not tell. The pain was too great to assess the damage. Besides, I felt that a broad and stoic smile was necessary to reassure the concerned onlookers who rushed to my aid.

The first person to reach me was a stranger from the next table. He bent over to lift me and I cried out to stop him. 'Please, it's my back – please don't move me,' I insisted. I was frightened that more damage might be done, and I needed a moment to recover from the shock. This was how I found myself beside a now kneeling stranger, explaining in minute detail what I might have otherwise only shared with a friend. He listened carefully about the two years of back trouble; and how I had been offered an operation that had less than a fifty-fifty chance of success, and that might, if unsuccessful, have resulted in my having to spend the rest of my life in a wheelchair. I had prayed about the operation, and then declined it on the grounds that if the Lord kept me on my feet I would keep going, pain or no pain. At least I was still mobile, after a fashion.

Right at that moment, on the hard floor, my continued mobility felt seriously in question. Amazingly, the stranger was still listening – in fact, not only listening, but interested. More than that, there was something in his eyes that told me he had a great deal to say on the subject. 'Have you ever considered the laying on of hands?' he asked. I hesitated in answering, not because I was embarrassed, but because I was not sure how to tell this kind gentleman that I myself, when requested, had practised the ministry of divine healing for some years now. He filled the silence with another question, 'Do you believe in it?'

I told him then, and he smiled. I also knew that no matter how much or how often God works through us to heal another, we cannot do it for ourselves. There is something in the trusting of another, the letting go of independence, the admitting of our inadequacy, the co-operation with fellow Christians in the process, and the victory over the temptation to want to be self-sufficient, that is part of the healing process of God to his children.

'Shall we do it now?' he asked, and had his eyes closed in prayer even as I nodded. Paddy Monaghan, Dublin-born Roman Catholic and born-again Christian, raised his hand to an inch above the affected spot on the back of the Presbyterian deaconess from Belfast. I was aware of the warmth of his hand through the light summer clothing on my back, even though his hand did not touch me – but the floor was colder, and I felt little else. The prayer was short, and I knew God would answer as he had answered those faithful elders and minister many years ago when I was a child. Although I stood stiffly and felt sore, I did not doubt for a moment that my shotgun marriage to the pain was soon to be dissolved.

That night, I slept without waking. It was the first full night's sleep I had had since taking up residence in the strange bed. Previously, my initial waking moments each morning since the onset of the pain had consisted of slow, tortuous dragging of my legs to the floor, and several minutes of bracing myself for the pain before slowly stretching to a standing position and clothing myself in prayer and agony before dressing for the day.

On this new day, I swung my legs out of bed and stood straight to my feet in one continuous movement, a movement that had not been possible for nearly two years. God had done it again; I was free once more. In joy and fruition I cried tears I had not allowed the pain to solicit on its own behalf. Then I found myself celebrating. I wanted to hug God; I just wanted to squeeze him so tight that all that glory cascaded around me – but I could not, because at the time he was too busy hugging me, and it felt so glorious.

LORD OF THE EAGLES

How shall I thank you, Lord of the eagles,
Gathering your chicks to the wing
Majesty soaring through heights unattainable,
Nurturing offspring in trust unexplainable,
Lavishing me now with love indefatigable,
How shall I thank you, my King?

How can I thank you
Master of hurting,
Turning my tears into praise,
For yours is the flowering of bough in mid-winter,
Yours the ripe harvest not wilting on vine,
Let the earth drink of the juice you would make of me,
Let them breathe deeply aroma that's mine.

17 EVEN IF THE SCENERY FALLS DOWN

During the International Year of the Disabled in 1981, I was honoured to represent Northern Ireland on the Regional Committee. 'How can we celebrate the year?' they asked me, 'what about writing a musical to communicate the problems of disability?' 'Why just the negatives?' I asked. 'What about the positives?'

Faces looked puzzled. 'Positives, what positives?' they asked. 'Well, can *you* park on a double yellow line and get away with it?' I retorted. I wasn't trying to encourage law breaking, but it was good to hear their laughter. Too often, disability is viewed as something to be 'cured' – a mistake, a problem, a burden. No one would wish a handicap upon anyone, but it should be the ability of each human being that is emphasised, not their disability. We need to stress what they are able to do, rather than their limitations. In able-bodied society, it would be a poor show indeed if conversation, judgements, and friendships revolved around the weaknesses and inadequacies of the others in our peer group, yet society often sees no inconsistency or injustice in highlighting, categorising, and emphasising those tasks/functions which a person finds difficult because of a physical, mental, or hidden disability – sometimes to the exclusion of proper recognition of their gifts, strengths, and talents.

Ability, not disability, was our slogan. I co-wrote the musical with Archy McNeill, one of Northern Ireland's most talented musicians and composers, and we called it *Freewheeler* – not 'freeloader', for I do not make any excuses or concessions for disability, but *Freewheeler* with its visual image of freewheeling in the fast lane, in style, wheels and all.

That year was quite a shock to my system. It was the year I discovered I was disabled. Oh yes, I had always known there were 'bits' of me that didn't work as well as they might, but I had never considered myself anything but 'normal'. I was raised in an atmosphere where I was treated normally, and expected to do everything my older sister did. From the beginning, I went everywhere the family went. If a task was difficult it was not done for me; I was expected to sweat that little bit harder, and put in as much extra effort as was required to get the job done, and done by myself without question. And sweat I did, constantly, and often literally. To me, the application of excessive exertion was a perfectly 'normal' requirement of living. Attending the ordinary state schools with 'ordinary' people, dreaming 'normal' dreams with 'normal' ambitions – accompanied by all the 'normal' frustrations, I had never considered myself different from the majority of the population. Suddenly I was asked to represent 'the disabled'.

Who were these strange and alien creatures that nobody considered 'normal'? Well, wonder of wonders, it wasn't long before I realised that it was not the people with disabilities who were off-centre, but rather all the attitudes which had coined words like 'normal' in the first place.

Even today, I laughingly tell audiences that 'I work with 'normal' people, but I can't find any.' It wasn't that I suddenly began to identify with some spurious 'disabled community' of which I had been previously unaware, but that I gained entrance to the human race – and found it to be a much wider category than I had previously imagined. How liberating it is to discover the truth in the adage that 'there's no such thing as normal'.

I had always related to 'people', and I still relate to 'people'. Never have I distinguished between the many categories contrived and invented by the world to control and segregate. I do not relate to disabled people more or less than able-bodied, and vice-versa. They are all just 'people', thank God.

My work is mainly with those labelled 'able-bodied', but, as a disabled person myself, I make sure that anyone whom society considers to fit that description is fully integrated into my groups/workshops/projects if they wish to be involved.

This is not a contrived policy; I do not run events for 'the disabled'. From my understanding of Scripture, Jesus' policy was fully integrationalist in a non-contrived manner. Human beings to him are basically human beings – 'For all have sinned, and come short of the glory of God' (Romans 3.23); 'There is neither Jew nor Greek, there is neither slave nor free, there is neither male nor female; for you are all one in Christ Jesus' (Galatians 3.28).

We had a cast of fifty for the musical. There were twenty-five able-bodied and twenty-five folk representing just about every type of disability imaginable, because I believed that it wasn't enough simply to *talk* about what we wanted to communicate. If something needs saying, 'Don't just talk about it, do it', I suggested to the Regional Committee, and they agreed wholeheartedly.

Blind, deaf, paraplegic, quadriplegic, incontinent, mentally handicapped, epileptic, diabetic, and a lot more besides, were the disabilities represented as fifty extremely hard-worked and exhausted persons made their entrance for the opening performance of a musical that subsequently toured the Province and was also invited to Dublin in a unique 'hands across the border' co-operative gesture for that special year.

Some of the audience told me later that, before they came, they could not have imagined such a cast singing and dancing at top speed through two-and-a-half hours of full-length musical without one person falling off the stage. I would smile at such comments, and think to myself under my breath, 'You should have seen the rehearsals!'

It was fun, but I think I aged ten years every week of the one-and-a-half years required to write, audition, cast, direct, and tour that musical. Nevertheless it was certainly worth it – and I thank God for the privilege of being allowed by him to be part of such an achievement. It might arguably be said that it was one of the most valuable learning experiences of my life. Laugh, we cried!

Like the rehearsal when, close to midnight and nothing going right, I was totally exhausted and still charging around at top speed. It was mid-winter, with two actors missing to receive their regular treatment in hospital, another stretched out backstage in pain from artificial limb chafing, another who could not remember a line all week, a fifth doing a prima donna act, and half the able-bodied cast in bed with flu. It was not a good night. Over and over, I had tried to impress upon the team how important it was to allow the disabled members of the cast not only to pull their weight, but, where possible, to be encouraged to take the lead. It was then, close to midnight, with my head in my hands, that I looked up to the stage to see big Sidney, tall as a house, blind, and built like a tank, heading at speed towards the edge of the stage with the entire case fastened on to each other's waists behind him, doing the best conga I had ever seen before or since.

I couldn't even shout a warning, for I was completely doubled up in fits of laughter. Sidney was leading the conga! It was too much even for me. Yet no one blinked an eyelid. He came within 2 inches of the edge, and deftly swung to the right with gaiety and poise, leading a now hooting-with-laughter fully integrated cast to safety upstage.

But that was nothing to the night, a few days into our opening week of performances at the Dalriada Theatre in the Ulster Polytec Jordanstown (as it was then), when someone missed a line. Now, it wasn't too bad, only one line, but the cue was missing for the next actor, and the show came to a brief halt. Only a few seconds' pause, mind you, before another actor saved the day. The audience hardly noticed. But the director noticed, I certainly did, and I was worried that it might happen again on another night in a more critical place, and then the whole performance would come to grief.

So after the show I gathered the troops for a briefing. 'Tomorrow night,' I boomed in my best sergeant-major's voice, 'you don't stop. I don't care *what* happens, you don't stop. Even if the scenery falls down, *you don't stop!*'

Well, have you ever wished that you had never spoken? The following evening, half-way through a big production number with the majority of the cast on-stage, one of the actors made a faster than usual entrance and in the process caught the edge of an 8-foot flat with his shoulder. It rocked slightly, and then began to topple. Directly in its path, two wheelchair users, a couple of blind actors, and several deaf dancers continued singing and dancing their hearts out – a few of them glancing only momentarily at the oncoming dead weight. The smiles, now cemented on, never left their faces, and the rest of the cast also continued as though nothing unusual was happening. Many of the audience were on their feet shouting warnings, or frozen in their seats drawing in their breath in horror. But on the stage, the show went on.

Desperately, I signalled from the wings for everyone to come off, yet no one moved. I suddenly remembered my words of the previous evening: 'I don't care *what* happens, you don't stop. Even if the scenery falls down, *you don't stop!*' It was like drowning. In those few seconds, it felt as if my whole life passed before my eyes. I had a sudden mental image of hurt bodies lying all across the stage moaning, whilst the rest danced round them. 'God, forgive me,' I prayed. 'They trust me to fix this; they're doing what I told them; please, God, PLEASE!'

Beside me in the wings, I caught a glimpse of Jim, a hefty male nurse who had endeared himself to the whole team, and was a valued asset to the musical – both medically and as a member of the cast. 'Jim,' I screamed, 'look!' I think he and several others backstage had already spotted the danger, because the speed at which they hurled themselves at the falling scenery saved the day. As they grabbed the back struts and returned the flat to an upright position, I peeped out at

WHAT NOISE DOES A PRAYER MAKE?

What noise does a prayer make,
When it rattles the pearly gates?
What noise does a God-thought make
As it wings its way to heaven?

What's the sound on the ground
Of a pound of whispers,
As it rattles
The registers of heaven?

What's the noise that the angels hear
As they politely stoop to incline the ear,
Do they ever find the line's none too clear
From static that's infernal?

Does the whee
    of a plea,
Or the click
    of a lick,
Or the smudge
    of a lie,
Or the sigh
    of a cry,
Ever vibrate the receivers eternal?

What noise does a prayer make,
As it rattles the pearly gates?
Does it shout,
Does it scream,
Does it know how to hold its breath
And to patiently,
     reverently,
     wait,
In awe of the one
Who might possibly come,
     swiftly,
To open the gate?

What sound falls upon the ear,
Of the maker who waits eager to hear
Every hope, every dream,
Each insult and fear
That spins, and twists,
And somersaults,
From earth to bliss.
I guess,
Whatever the sound may be,
The wish from heaven
Is simply that we,
Would break the radio silence.

18 THE MAKING OF EVE

It never fails to amaze me what God can do with rubbish. I mean, as a human, creative person, I delight to see beautiful things made out of fine materials, gold, silver, precious stones – but God, well, he's not fussed, is he? Any old dollop of mud will do the job. I suppose it is because the beauty is within his will and his fingers; it is not conditioned by the limitations inherent in the substance of the material with which he chooses to work.

In 1988, for Telethon, I was asked to paint a mural on television that was 7 feet high and 24 feet long, and it was my privilege to involve several hundred young people from youth clubs on either side of the divide to make up the painting rota. The theme was the six days of creation, and we made it tactile. Every bit of rubbish we could find was used: egg boxes for the tortoise, cotton wool for the clouds, and real feathers for the birds – which we had gathered from beaches around Ireland. (The feathers had already been discarded by their previous owners, I hasten to add.) It was quite an amazing masterpiece in rubbish – almost as amazing as the conversations constantly generated by many of the 'artists' as they toiled long and hard, some of them in the wee small hours of the morning, alongside those of 'the other sort', never before met. Disabled folk also became involved, and young offenders on remand.

On the opening evening of the programme, I stood nervously in front of the long stretch of plywood which, by faith, I believed would become the mural, awaiting my cue for the opening interview representing Northern Ireland in the nation-wide Telethon project. Beside and around me were gathered my core team of artists from the Art College, who helped so generously with their time and talents to design and sketch a foundation pattern upon which the others could work. The television company had decoratively positioned attractive pots of plants along the floor between us and the mural, tastefully screening out all the pots of paint and rubbish necessary for the creative process. The plant pots were joined by pretty – but (as it proved) disastrously low-lying – chains, to prevent the public who crowded into the marquee as an audience from tramping all over the artists' materials. However, no one had reckoned on a small emergency arising prior to the final few moments of countdown to Northern Ireland going nation-wide with my interview.

The floor manager was holding everyone in readiness; each person was tense in an enjoyable kind of excitement. Everyone had their eyes upon the monitor – all, that is, except one of the television technicians, who needed to extradite himself from behind the plants in front of the mural and directly to my rear. He had been dutifully fixing a last-minute problem with the framework of the mural and was concerned to find himself threatening to be 'in shot' as the final countdown was engaged. Quick-thinking and nimble, he took a short cut and leapt over the plant pots. Unfortunately, he hadn't reckoned on those low-lying chains linking each pot. As his toe caught on one of them, over went the plant beside me, setting off an exquisitely executed domino effect. On to the ground spilled soil, plants, paint, and everything. With less than a minute to go, the studio around my feet looked like a disaster area.

To the credit of the television staff, I have never seen people move so quickly; it was professionalism at its very best. I was also extremely proud of my own team who flung themselves at the mess. Handfuls of soil were crammed anywhere and everywhere possible: down blouses, up trousers, kicked behind the mural, stuffed into handbags. My Multi-Media Workshop costume designer and general emergency 'Mrs Fix-it' of twenty years, Mrs Sandra Ferguson, worked so fast that I am hard put to be convinced she didn't eat the half of it. Whatever she and the others did, as the floor manager held up the final three fingers, the floor and surrounding area was immaculate. As the camera light lit for me, I am sure many an artist closed fists tightly and prayed that tiny little granules of soil would not be seen trickling from the palms of their hands. I daresay it would have served to make it look even more interesting for the viewers. After all, we were doing the six days of creation, weren't we?

Thank the Lord that the potential of his human creation is not conditional upon the state of the material with which he has to work. I am sure Adam and Eve were grateful for that – I know I am.

THE MAKING OF EVE

Grubbing in the dust
He found the mud a trifle squelchy
Found the ribs a little brittle,
Found the rib that needed taking,
For the mould that needed breaking,
Recycled, not forsaken
For the she that He was making.

Wading through the mud
He found the clay a little cracked
Found the dirt a little grubby,
Found the dirt that grows the earth-life,
Placed the seed of His own mirth life,
Re-united joy with sorrow
For the she He deemed was worth life.

Dancing to the sea
He found the light would sparkle radiant
Found the waves would flow succinctly,
Found an ebb tide just her colour
For a leader, thinker, mother,
Uniquely stamped His image
To present her to the other.

Weeping by the pool
He found her eyes reflecting distance,
Found the pain that hid the future,
Found the pain that pierced Him also,
For how sword from sickle grows
Lies not within the earth plan
Such knowledge only reptile shows.

Standing by the tree
He found the glimpse into her future,
Found the tears she'd weep beside Him,
Found the wood to carve their death stake,
For the she He'd made for God's sake
Heart pierced and womb re-kindled
Soon would cradle Him for earth's sake.

Grubbing in the dust
He found the mud a trifle squelchy,
Found the hearts a little brittle,
Found the hearts that needed taking,
For the world that needed making,
Re-born not unforgiven
Those who bear the name of women.

19 PRICELESS MOMENT

I had never thought much about being a woman. Oh yes, on all those forms needing to be filled in on my way through life I had always dutifully marked an 'F' in the gender box, so I did not need telling I was a member of the 'fair' sex. But I always considered my body to be a vehicle to move around the earth in, and – let's face it – as a vehicle, it was at times a poor means of transport.

The Boss, however, has greater ambitions for us than that we should simply learn how to negotiate road signs and garage ourselves safely in the shed each night. Miracle of miracles, he made us physical beings, as much as creatures of intellect and spirit. It is within his gift to humankind that we should become not only healed, but whole. I had not yet fully realised this when, in 1980, I discovered the lump in my breast.

I first discovered it while in the bath – just a tiny thing, hardly worth bothering about, I thought. It was my busiest and most successful year yet, professionally speaking. I was in the midst of preparations for the *Freewheeler* musical for the International Year of the Disabled, and committed to an extremely full schedule of rehearsals, organising, forward planning, motivating, and directing. Everything threatened the project's demise, with many people predicting that it would never work.

There were long, arduous rehearsals, and recurring bouts of illness in the cast. It was necessary to write and rewrite the script again and again, to accommodate those persons missing through no fault of their own – sometimes even having to scribble a hasty rewrite as near to 'curtain-up' as half-an-hour before the performance, because of a last-minute dropout.

There was also the lack of transport in getting folk to and from rehearsal venues, when my Ford Escort had to take on the proportions of an estate wagon and the mileage of a troop carrier. When I come to think of it, the whole project had to be conducted like a military manoeuvre, especially when we began the performances which went on tour from Derry to Dublin. Meantime, my regular duties as a deaconess continued unabated. What with all this and frequent television appearances and radio broadcasts for interviews about the musical and the Year in general, not to mention serving on the Regional Committee for the entire year of projects, I did not have time to find a lump in my breast.

But there it was: small, and potentially deadly. I sobbed with my Lord; I yelled at him. 'I haven't time, Lord,' I screamed. 'Not this year, not now.' Yet the lump would not go away, and neither would God's quiet insistence that I go and have it examined. Eventually, I went. Once the performances were over in early 1981, when the applause had died, at the end of a unique example of teamwork, and the curtain closed on fifty dynamic, smiling, exuberantly successful actors who had given 110 per cent, and had proved, in God's strength, that all things are possible, I walked from the stage and into the cancer-screening unit at my local health centre.

'*Please*, God, let it be nothing,' I pleaded. I was referred to the hospital for tests. It was hard having everyone I met in the waiting-room greet me with: 'You're Hilary McDowell, aren't you?', 'We've seen you on TV', 'The musical was great', 'Keep up the good work'. Then the worst question of all, 'What are you doing here?'

I smiled and shook hands, and told stories of our performances, when all the time I felt like dying inside. I was scared and felt terribly alone. For the first time in my life, the woman in me refused to be ignored. Part of her, a very feminine part of her, a pretty part, a healthy, attractive, non-disabled, non-disfigured, *normal*, part of her, was under terrible threat. She would not go away – I tried to quiet her with busyness, but the long hours in the many waiting-rooms forced me to think. I tried to deafen her with prayers as I lay down to sleep, but she kept begging God louder than my intellect, louder than my mind, louder, it seemed, even than my soul. 'Don't let me lose it, Lord,' I screamed, 'please take something else, anything – take a leg, they've never worked properly anyway, but don't take this, dear God, don't take this from me, I'm a *woman!*' Categorically, I knew then that that's what I was, and so did God.

No one seemed to understand. Worst of all were the well-meaning ones who tried. My family were going about with the proverbial 'stiff upper lip', and pretending there was nothing to worry about. For their sakes, I pretended too, and those months I learnt more 'of the dying'. Thank the Lord I had good friends, who did their best to take my mind off things. Thank you, Robin, for keeping me company during the worst of the times, and Helen, a nurse, who walked with me closely in the final days up to the operation. But none could go into the operating theatre with me. No other person but myself could sign the form that gave sanction to – to what? No one else could stand before Jesus and surrender even this wonderful, beautiful, feminine part of me to the Saviour and say, 'This too, Lord, is yours; thy will be done.'

Before the exploratory operation to ascertain whether the lump was benign or malignant, I sought the advice of an old friend and renowned surgeon, William Rutherford, whose life and work in Northern Ireland is a wonderful Christian witness to all. I remember standing in his surgery and blurting out that I didn't want to stop being a woman. It seems a basic and banal statement now, but it had taken a whole lifetime until then to acknowledge my femininity and my need to meet the needs of that aspect of my being. It felt cruel justice indeed to be faced with this realisation so close to the possibility of relinquishing something so precious and so vital to my newly discovered identity. At that point in time, my breast was the most precious thing in the world to me, because I was in danger of losing it. Dr Rutherford did not preach or pontificate. He neither blinded me with science, nor ignored my need to know every technical detail. He answered when I asked questions, but most of all he listened – and especially, he shared my tears. Crying with him as a child with a father, I knew again how much God loved me. I knew once more that I had to exercise complete trust. On the way home, I remembered my mother's words – 'Hilary, God hasn't brought you this far to desert you now' – and my father's conversation a few months before God called him home, although he was in no way ill and no one had prior warning of his sudden death: 'I'm proud of you, Hilary, you've done the things I would have done if I could. God has trusted us both all the way. He's never let me down, nor you either.'

I prayed that night, and read again a poem I had written as a teenager which ends, 'He had faith in you, girl, enough to give you life.' I went into the hospital remembering it, but I was scared, not of death, but of what else I might lose in life.

The side room was private, if a little old-fashioned, inside the ancient walls of the Royal Victoria Hospital, Belfast, the night that I prepared for the exploratory operation. It is a famous hospital with a first-class reputation. Some years before offering my application as a deaconess candidate, I had worked in this hospital in the purchasing department, ordering the sterile supplies and equipment for the wards. I remembered the forms I had processed, the pacemakers and assorted instruments that it had been the department's responsibility to keep on supply and available. As I got ready for bed, I wondered if any of the sterile supplies I had ordered would be used tomorrow morning on me. I laughed; it seemed a surrealistic notion, and I pushed it from my mind. At least, I mused, I was laughing – but not for long.

The bed was very high and the floor was stone cold; the light had to be switched out at the door. Attempting to walk in bare feet is something akin to ice skating for me, and that light switch was some distance away. I was in pyjamas and ready for bed, feeling both tired and afraid. Trying to trust with a mixture of trust and fear all rolled into one, I thought, 'What will I do, Lord, if I struggle to the door to turn the light off, and I can't get back to the too-high bed in the dark without slippers.' When you're at the end of your tether, the smallest inconvenience takes on enormous proportions, and that single straw is sufficient to break the camel's back.

In reality, there would have been many things I could have done: a team of nurses to call; slippers to put on again only a hand's distance away; I might even have chosen to leave the light on if I had wanted. Yet the straw was loaded, and the camel's back was broken in the desert. I flung myself across the bottom of the bed an arm's length from the light switch at the door, my feet dragging on the ice-cold flooring, and let the tears flow. I sobbed enough for a lifetime. They were a lifetime's backlog of female needs, and God knew they needed crying.

I cannot tell how long I cried, but it was very, very late when I was all cried out. Exhausted, I dreaded the pitch blackness that I imagined would swamp the room if I managed to gain the composure to flick off the light switch. I lay still for a moment, all cried to pieces but no less afraid. I prayed; I clearly remember the words I used. It was a very short prayer – I was too physically exhausted for more: 'Be with me Lord in the darkness'. I whispered it fearfully, and then dragged myself the few extra inches to the door.

The switch clicked off and the room was plunged instantly into the luminous glow of bright moonlight from a skylight-type window opposite the bed. It was a glorious shock. I could see every detail of the room as though in daylight. I was surprised; I was jubilant. God had done it again; he was laughing with me. Standing there, in bare feet, on a chill floor, in my pyjamas, awaiting that operation, God took me in his arms again, not only lovingly, but laughingly, and to-gether he and I laughed, and laughed and laughed. It was neither sweet reason nor theology that God used to comfort me that night, but a simple and very practical meeting of my need for light in the darkness, and he did it with a sense of humour. I slept peacefully, by moonlight.

It was necessary, as with all operations, to sign a consent form beforehand. I refused to take pre-med or agree to sign the form for this exploratory operation until I had been brought either a typewriter or a pen to amend one of the clauses before signing. God, I believed, would do his part to save me from the worst. I, for my part, believed I had to take responsibility for what consequently happened to my body. I did not believe that a team of doctors, no matter how competent, should have to carry the devastating responsibility for such a decision. I was allowed to amend the clause, and continued to the theatre. The agreement was that, whatever was discovered – whether benign or malignant – I would be awakened and told the situation before anything was done. Then I would be allowed to make the decision myself as to whether to have further surgery or not.

As the brilliant surgeon Odling Smee, himself a committed Christian, and his team prepared me in the theatre, I remember lying stretched out awaiting the injection muttering, 'I'll be praying for you.' They made no reply as they worked; I expect they thought I was under the influence of the pre-med, but I was fully aware of what I was saying and why I said it. I knew God was at their side working through them as they operated, and I thank God for such skilled and dedicated professionals.

I came out of the anaesthetic in the recovery ward, with the nursing sister slapping me gently on the cheek and proclaiming quite loudly, 'It's all right, Hilary, all's clear.' I was not fully in charge of my senses. I tried to raise my head to question her, but it fell weakly back on to the pillow. 'What,' I pleaded, 'What!' 'It's all right, Hilary,' she repeated. 'The results are back from the lab. It was an innocent wee thing, nothing to worry about.'

I collapsed into healing sleep again. When I awoke later, I

was back in the ward and doubting everything I had heard. Had I been imagining it, I wondered? Was the sister a dream, did she really say it was all right? Trembling again with nervousness and fear, I called for a nurse. 'Is it true?' I quizzed, trying to read the expression on her face. 'I think I remember hearing the sister, but I might have imagined it. Is it true, is everything all right?' The young nurse disappeared immediately and brought back several experts. They gathered around the bed, and their smiles were evidence enough of the pleasure they had in confirming the good news. Not only was the lump benign, but my breast was unmarked and unchanged – except for a small wound which Mr Smee had closed with such meticulously tiny stitches that, within a short time, not even a scar was left. My breast was saved, but more – much more – than that, I walked from the hospital a *whole* person: body, mind, and spirit. Fully healed and completely a woman.

PRICELESS MOMENT

For each of us
The most precious thing in the world
Is that which we are in danger of losing,
> a job,
> a marriage,
> a breast,
> a child,
It differs on every
> slow day,
> fast day,
> birthday,
> anniversary,
Only on our death day
Do we believe we are in danger of losing our soul,
Priceless moment – too late.

20 PREPARATION FOR FLIGHT

Everything that happens to us on earth is flight preparation. I believe this both from my own experience of living, and also from what the Bible teaches me. Jesus said, 'I came that they might have life, and have it abundantly' (John 10.10).

This flying needs no wings. When I penned the title poem of this book many years ago, I had little idea what course my life would take, yet I knew then what I know still: that my life is a challenge or it is nothing. When Jesus spoke of life more abundantly, he was talking of life, not survival. When I think of flight, it is not earthly ambition or success that I envisage, but spiritual vision. It is God who has walked close within my pain; and eternal life is not just in heaven, but is meant to begin now upon earth when we commit our lives to Jesus Christ and make him our Lord. As we struggle through life, there are so many circumstances that can threaten to weld our gaze to the pavement: illness, fears, past memories, losses, and hurts of every kind can narrow our gaze and impose upon us tunnel vision, where we can see only the next problem on the horizon. Lurching from one emergency to the next, enmeshed in the turmoil of the instant need, we can lose sight of the journey which we travel. Dwelling within the immediate moment is good if that means not harping back to yesterday, or longing for a perfect tomorrow which will not come. But if dwelling in the present moment becomes for us slavery to every immediate demand, then our gaze will become welded to the pavement and we will never be able to lift our eyes to the distant horizon.

Without God, I could not take another breath, nor would I want to live without his joy in my life and his power in my every step. He has walked close within my pain and brought rejoicing – not in place of sorrow, but often in the midst of it. His touch enlivens my life – not in spite of difficulties, but often because of them.

This person who allows me to call him 'Boss' also lets me call him 'Abba' – Daddy. It is because he loves us that he answers our prayers, and because he loves us entirely that he does not always give us what we want. He is not a Santa Claus to read our shopping-list prayers and deliver every whim, whether it is good for us or not. Just imagine the adult equivalent of ten gross of sweets dropped down the chimney tied with a bow and without any discrimination as to whether or not the gift will rot our teeth. We like to think humankind is more mature than that, until we examine some of the self-centred requests made to the Creator.

When happiness is often thought to encapsulate such luxuries as lack of pain, exemption from suffering, material success, freedom from trouble, fulfilment of our human plans (the list is endless), it is little wonder that he receives some very odd prayer requests. Often we settle for second-best by insisting on getting our own way, when he can see the overall picture of our lives and wishes only the *very best* for us.

That is why God has given us a much better prayer than any we can think up by ourselves. It includes the phrase 'Thy will be done' (Matthew 6.10). In praying this phrase with each of our requests to God, we are trusting a mind infinitely greater than our own, an infallible visionary whose dreams are both practical and loving. He sees past, present, and future simultaneously. He knows what plans he has for you, and, most reassuringly, he is not ignorant of a single one of our defects, sins, or weaknesses, and loves us, in spite of them, with an unconditional love.

God has answered all of my prayers. Some he has answered with a 'Yes', some with a 'No', and many more with a gentle touch and a whisper of 'Wait awhile'. The last of the three kinds of answer is the hardest to bear, for it requires a person to exercise trust. When I trust him, I discover that God is neither a Santa Claus nor a magician. He doesn't wave a magic wand and make it all different, but he will take a committed life and make it all possible. But I also know that God is not some impersonal dictator watching us from a distance and I know this because of Jesus. No one could accuse him of standing far away, and watching us with detachment – no one who knows of the cross, that is. Jesus got involved with Earth on an extremely personal level and is still prepared to be involved, person to person, with individuals today.

I have tried to express these twin truths about God in the words of the final trilogy of poems which conclude this book. Not only the humanity of a personal God whom we can see in the nature of Jesus, but also an all-powerful monarch of the universe whose bear-hug would 'break every bone in your soul'.

It is impossible to be touched by God and not be changed, but his aim is an 'improved model', not a rehashed mess. His ambitions for our relationship with him makes our faint prayers for improvement of our life on earth look like wishes to win a tiddlywinks contest. The bad news (as we sometimes see it) is that he is designing a workout that will put us in the World Cup class of players. The good news is that it is a trophy worth attaining – a victory worth winning. It has been won for us by Christ himself, and we are invited to enter into partnership with him in the continuing creative work of the Trinity throughout all eternity.

God's search for partners has always been urgent. First, we must give in our notice in our present occupation: that of 'getting by on earth as best we can with ourselves as the centre of our own universe', and apply for 'sonship (and daughtership) of the Kingdom'. According to the Bible, it has to be a conscious choice on our part. God does not force a relationship on us.

A new identity requires a new birth, and only by repentance of the past, no matter how small or large the mistakes we feel we have made or the sins committed, and by acceptance of the Lord Jesus Christ as Saviour and Master, can we begin the spiritual journey that God initiated when he 'formed you in the womb' (Jeremiah 1.5). Each one of us enters this world as his created child and then he waits for us to choose him as Lord of our lives. On the day I made that choice, life did not stop being an uphill struggle but it has continued ever since as real life, not survival.

I thank the Lord for making me; all that I see in the mirror is his. I long to fulfil his purpose for my life. It is an ongoing challenge and a long journey but the power is God's, he has placed me on the runway – and some day I'm going to fly.

TRINITY PICTURES

FATHER

Mud moulding,
Thunder cracking,
Rainbow-painting,
Reality,
He called you
'Abba',
May I call you
'Dad'?
I don't forget though
    that those who play
    with lightning—
Get their fingers scorched.
    Don't you imagine that
    a bear's hug from a God
Would break every bone
    in your soul?

SON

Don't you suppose that
    a regular, card-
    carrying member
    of the human race
Would cry a little?
JESUS WEPT—
    And that's not all!

SPIRIT

Touch me,
Touching
You.
WHITE HEAT,
Like
A dove.

Also available from
Tri/\ngle

OUT OF THE ORDINARY
Calligraphy and Meditations

A delightful series of meditations on everyday objects. From a cup
to a flower to a table, Anthea Dove enables her readers to find
God's blessings in the ordinary stuff of life.

Includes calligraphy by Christina Caldwell

Books by Frank Colquhoun
and published by
Tri/\ngle

PRAYERS FOR TODAY

A modern book of prayers dealing with matters of common
experience. Divided into three sections, the prayers cover
personal life, the Christian pilgrimage and a broad range of public
issues. Many of the prayers are also suitable for use in church or
group worship.

PRAYERS FOR EVERYONE

A wide-ranging collection offering prayers for many different
situations. Prayers of Christian faith and devotion are gathered
together with some for everyday needs and others showing a
concern for the world around us. The book also includes a special
section of Celtic material.

FAMILY PRAYERS

Prayers and thanksgivings for all family occasions – from times of
joy or of sadness; of celebration or of change; from the birth of a
new baby to the loss of a grandparent. There are also prayers for
friends, neighbours, the local community and the church
fellowship.

Also available from
Tri△ngle

Books by David Adam

THE EDGE OF GLORY
Prayers in the Celtic tradition

Modern prayers which recapture the Celtic way of intertwining
divine glory with the ordinariness of everyday events.

THE CRY OF THE DEER
Meditations on the Hymn of St Patrick

Meditations leading to practical exercises which take us deeper in
to the prayer experience in affirming the Presence of God.

TIDES AND SEASONS
Modern prayers in the Celtic tradition

A series of prayers which echo the rhythms of creation, finding
their parallels in our spiritual lives and in the highs and lows of
all human experience.

THE EYE OF THE EAGLE
Meditations on the hymn 'Be thou my vision'

David Adam takes us through the words of the Celtic hymn, 'Be
thou my vision', discovering the spiritual riches that are hidden
in all our lives.

POWER LINES
Celtic prayers about work

A series of modern prayers about work which incorporate the
insights of the Celtic tradition. The book opens up Celtic
patterns of prayer to focus on the work we all do in the presence
of God.

The PRAYING WITH series

A series of books making accessible the words of some of the great
characters and traditions of faith for use by all Christians. There
are 14 titles in the series, including:

PRAYING WITH SAINT AUGUSTINE
Introduction by Murray Watts

PRAYING WITH SAINT FRANCIS
Introduction by David Ford

PRAYING WITH THE NEW TESTAMENT
Introduction by Joyce Huggett

PRAYING WITH SAINT TERESA
Introduction by Elaine Storkey

PRAYING WITH THE OLD TESTAMENT
Introduction by Richard Holloway

PRAYING WITH THE ENGLISH MYSTICS
Compiled and Introduced by Jenny Robertson

PRAYING WITH THE ENGLISH POETS
Compiled and Introduced by Ruth Etchells

PRAYING WITH THE MARTYRS
Preface by Madeleine L'Engle

PRAYING WITH JOHN DONNE AND GEORGE HERBERT
Preface by Richard Harries

TriΛNGlE
Books
can be obtained from all good bookshops.
In case of difficulty, or for a complete
list of our books, contact:
SPCK Mail Order
36 Steep Hill,
Lincoln LN2 1LU
(tel: 01522 527 486)